Chronology of Immigration
in the United States

Chronology of Immigration in the United States

RUSSELL O. WRIGHT

McFarland & Company, Inc., Publishers

Jefferson, North Carolina, and London

LIBRARY OF CONGRESS CATALOGUING-IN-PUBLICATION DATA

Wright, Russell O.
    Chronology of immigration in the United States / Russell
O. Wright.
        p.   cm.
    Includes bibliographical references and index.

    ISBN: 978-0-7864-3627-9
    softcover : 50# alkaline paper ∞

    1. United States — Emigration and immigration — Chronology.
I. Title.
JV6450.W76   2008
304.8'7300202 — dc22   2008005372

British Library cataloguing data are available

On the cover: Immigrants from the *Prinzess Irene* at Ellis Island
(Library of Congress); baggage ©2008 Shutterstock

Manufactured in the United States of America

McFarland & Company, Inc., Publishers
    Box 611, Jefferson, North Carolina 28640
        www.mcfarlandpub.com

To Mary Emma Wright MacWhorter

Acknowledgments

As with my previous books in this series, what I have designated as the "Wright writing company" played a major part in the generation of this book.

My wife, Halina K. Wright, served both as editor and researcher for this book (not to mention she provided technical assistance when my computer wouldn't do what I wanted it to do compared to what I may have told it to do).

My daughter, Terry A. Wright, prepared the manuscript for submission and created the index and other parts of the book. Her expertise with Microsoft Word is fortunately matched by her expertise in surfing the Internet and finding not only the most obscure information but the latest version of the data quoted throughout the book and in the appendices. This latter ability plays a major role in reducing the degree to which parts of any reference book are outdated by the time it is published.

Further extending the family nature of the Wright writing company was a Father's Day gift of a marvelous new printer just at the time it was urgently needed. My son, Brian K. Wright, set up the printer and added other components so that it could be used with my truly ancient (in computer time) equipment. Terry, of course, was the key to operating the printer at its full capabilities and producing the entire manuscript in the wink of an eye.

This is my nineteenth book, and never has the Wright writing company played a larger part in creating one of my books than it did in this one.

Table of Contents

Introduction

Immigration involves the movement of people from one country to another with the intent of establishing a permanent residence in the new country. The people who immigrate are called immigrants whereas people who leave a country to migrate to another country emigrate and are known as emigrants.

Immigration has occurred on a worldwide basis for centuries, but the primary movement since 1600 involved nearly 70 million people who left Europe for other countries. About 40 million of these people came to the United States. This book is a chronology of the events concerning the immigration of these 40 million plus another 40 million who have come from all over the world (legally and illegally) to the United States in just the last 75 years. This total of 80 million is still growing at a rate that exceeds one million people each year.

The United States is truly a nation of immigrants. It was very sparsely populated in 1600 (mostly by Native American Indians), but today it is a nation of about 300 million, nearly all of whom are immigrants or descendents of immigrants. There are other countries that have grown since 1600 primarily by an influx of immigrants, such as Argentina and Australia to name just two notable examples. However, immigrants to Australia (present population about 20 million) have been about 80 percent British, and immigrants to Argentina (present population about 40 million) have been about 75 percent Italian and Spanish. Immigrants to the United States have come from around the globe, with different countries providing the greatest number of immigrants at different times. Yearly immigration to the

Introduction

United States is still counted in the millions, while in most countries immigration is a minor factor in population growth, if such growth occurs at all.

Immigrants have come to the United States for many reasons, including the most obvious one of seeking economic improvements in their lives. There are many stories, perhaps over-romanticized, of people coming to the United States seeking religious freedom or escaping political tyranny in their country of origin, but however poignant these stories may be on an individual basis, estimates are that historically 90 percent of all immigrants to the United States have come for economic reasons and only 10 percent have come for political or religious reasons. That remains true today.

Another perhaps over-romanticized story, even to the point of being a myth, is that people in the United States generously welcomed all immigrants and that only in recent decades have there been "problems" with immigrants. The actuality is that even though the Declaration of Independence in 1776 and the original Constitution of the United States a decade later encouraged immigration to the new country, immigration has been viewed as a problem to the residents of the United States even before it was officially a new country.

Since colonial times, there has been economic pressure on the early settlers to encourage immigration to provide labor (and even simply to increase the number of settlers). Other than slaves from Africa, immigrants came voluntarily to America, mostly, as noted, to improve their own economic situation. The move meant the possibility of eventually owning land, which was important to many immigrants. Early on, the immigrants included many indentured servants who traded passage to America and a certain number of years of labor after arrival for the opportunity to become free men and landowners in the future.

Thus, many new immigrants worked menial, labor-intensive jobs and were looked down on by those already here. The new immigrants often had different cultural backgrounds and were derided because they "couldn't speak English." Until each new group became assimilated into American culture, they were looked on as outsiders. Then newly assimilated group eventually looked down on the next wave of new immigrants in the same way had been looked down on when they originally arrived.

There were always tensions in the general population which viewed immigrants as a necessary evil, but one that continually put downward pressure on prevailing wages. Eventually, as will be detailed in this chronology, official immigration policies were developed in the new nation called the United States to prevent certain types of immigrants from entering the country at all.

This means that there were immigration "problems" from the time of the colonial settlers (who actually made up only a small proportion of the early population in America) onward. As the number of immigrants swelled into the millions by the 19th century, the number of problems increased. But the basic problem was always the same. The country needed new immigrants primarily to make up a cheap labor force (especially for menial and undesirable work), but there were always arguments about which immigrants were "desirable" or "undesirable," and there were also concerns about certain immigrant groups "taking over" the country. These problems have existed for five centuries and still exist today, but the groups of immigrants involved have changed.

In order to put today's problems in context, the rest of this introduction provides a brief overview of immigration to the United States since 1600. It discusses a forecast of what will happen in immigration in the near future. A chronology of key events beginning with the 1600s is the main part of the book.

The Colonial Period (1600–1775)

The first permanent colonial English settlement in America was made in 1607 at Jamestown, Virginia. Colonists settled around the Chesapeake Bay and established a profitable business growing tobacco for sale to a ready market in Europe. Growing tobacco was highly labor intensive, and petty criminals from England were some of the indentured servants who came to meet the need for labor.

The first blacks from Africa were brought to Jamestown in 1619, and although they may have been brought as indentured servants, subsequent black laborers were brought as slaves. By the late 1600s slaves were seen as essential to the tobacco-based economy. This view spread to other agricultural products in the south (especially cotton) and the slave trade grew

Introduction

throughout the 17th and 18th centuries. The international slave trade was finally declared illegal in 1808 as per the constitution twenty years earlier (the existing domestic slave trade was not disturbed), but about 50,000 slaves were smuggled into the United States after 1808 through the 1850s. Thus, in a sense, the first "illegal immigrants" flooded the United States during the first half of the 19th century. The sequence was as it would always be afterwards. Certain businessmen who wanted the cheap labor of the illegals were willing to pay whatever it took in whatever form was required to enable the "illegals" to enter the country. After the end of the Civil War in 1865, there were about 4.5 million former slaves and their descendents who became new citizens of the United States. They accounted for 13.5 percent of the total population at that time.

Immigration to the New England area began in 1620 with the famous landing at Plymouth Rock by the *Mayflower*. The settlers were known as Pilgrims and were basically seeking religious freedom lacking in England, their country of origin. However, a larger settlement of so-called English Puritans arrived in Massachusetts Bay in 1629, and more than 20,000 others arrived in the following decade. It was the Puritans who shaped the initial culture of Massachusetts and even to some degree the culture of the colonies overall.

The Puritans were strictly religious, and believed in hard work and education. Some of them owned slaves in the 17th and 18th centuries, but slavery never played a prominent role in New England economic life, and the New England states eventually took the lead in making slavery illegal in the United States. But however strong their Protestant Christian faith, the Puritans were opposed to certain kinds of immigrants. The Puritans recognized a Christian obligation to help the poor among them, but only the "deserving" poor. They had a practice of "warning off" newcomers they felt were "undesirable" and who might become dependent on public charity. Warning off meant exactly what it sounds like. Undesirable newcomers were told to move on and to not try to absorb resources from the hard-working citizens already living in the town. Further, other "undesirables" such as Jews were sent away regardless of their personal resources. Again, immigration problems existed very early in the life of the new country.

In addition to the settlers from England, settlers from the Netherlands and Sweden established settlements along the Atlantic Coast between

Jamestown and Boston. The Dutch formed the colony of New Nether-lands in 1614, and built New Amsterdam (eventually to become New York) in 1626. But following an ongoing series of wars with Great Britain in the 1600s, the Dutch finally ceded their establishments to the English in 1664. Sweden founded the colony of New Sweden in 1638 around what is now Delaware, but their colony was absorbed by the Dutch in 1655 and then turned over to the English when the Dutch gave way to Great Britain. The Dutch and Swedish colonies were quite cosmopolitan for their time, but essentially they just gave the English a bigger piece of the new continent along the Atlantic Coast.

William Penn was given land by King Charles II in 1681, and Penn went on to found Pennsylvania, whose major city Philadelphia was the largest in the colonies up to the time of the revolution in 1776. Philadel-phia's most famous citizen was Benjamin Franklin, writer, publisher, sci-entist, diplomat, and leader who helped develop the Declaration of Independence in 1776. It is much less well known that Franklin was a ded-icated Nativist, that is, a person who is opposed to an internal minority on the basis that the minority is "un–American." Twenty-five years before the welcoming words in the Declaration of Independence he helped put together, Franklin had written of his disgust with the German immigrants who flooded into Philadelphia and the Pennsylvania area in general. He found them to "herd together," to refuse to adapt to existing customs, and to speak German in an attempt to "take over" and have Americans speak their language rather than their learning to speak English. It was a com-plaint that continues today. He also wanted a "purely white" America (con-sisting only of the English and some Saxon Germans in his opinion), and he was opposed to African blacks and also "swarthy" Europeans. It was not an uncommon complaint at the time, but the point is that ill will toward who are "different" is definitely not a recent development.

The French and the Spanish also founded colonies in America dur-ing the pre–Revolutionary period. The Spanish claimed the first Euro-pean colony in America in St. Augustine, Florida, in 1565. But Spain was a power that would enter a period of decline in the next few centuries. Although it once claimed large portions of land in what is now Mexico and the southwestern United States, Spain would cede independence to Mexico in 1821, and Texas would break away from Mexico in 1836, and then join the United States in 1845. Most of Mexico's remaining claims in the southwestern United States would be taken over by the United States in a one-sided war-ending treaty in 1848. Immigration issues with Mexico (and Puerto Rico and the Philippines, both taken from Spain in the war of 1898) would not become substantial until the 20th century. France would claim most of the United States west of the Mississippi, and make much trouble in the 17th century with its alliances with Native American Indians, but President Thomas Jefferson would buy the French interests in 1803, essentially doubling the size of the United States and eliminating any future immigration issues with the French in one stroke. Thus, the English-controlled colonies basically set the rules of immigration to America prior to the Revolutionary War of 1775–1783.

The governing British had very few restrictions on people wanting to immigrate to their colonies in North America. Most immigrants came from Great Britain, but they also came from nearly every part of Western Europe. It is estimated that in 1690 there were a little more then 200,000 people in the colonies. By the time of the Revolutionary War (hostilities actually started in 1775 in New England before the Declaration of Independence in 1776), there were about 2.5 million people in the colonies. In addition to the natural increase of the original colonists and settlers (and slaves), from 1700 to 1775 about 260,000 additional African slaves were brought to the United States. Slaves made up about 22 percent of the population by 1775. Other notable immigrants during the 1700–1775 period included 50,000 white convicts brought (usually as indentured servants) from England, 80,000 Scots-Irish from Ireland, and 70,000 Germans.

1775 to 1840

At the time of the American Revolution (from the start of hostilities in New England rather than the 1776 Declaration of Independence), the population of 2.5 million in the United States consisted of more than 500,000 slaves, 250,000 Scots-Irish, and 200,000 Germans, among its largest "immigrant" groups. The rest were immigrants as well, or the descendents of original immigrants since 1600. After the war officially ended in 1783 (the winning battle took place in 1781), the United States put together a constitution and elected its first president, George Washington, who took office in 1789. With a population of nearly 4 million, the nation began to focus on immigration issues in the 1790s.

Congress passed a law in 1790 requiring a two-year residency period before an immigrant could qualify for citizenship. The residency period was raised to five years in 1795. During the presidency of John Adams, who became president in 1796, the so-called Alien and Sedition Acts were passed in 1798. These consisted of four acts that among other things extended the period of residency required for citizenship to 14 years and gave the president authority to expel any foreigner residing in the United States thought to be threatening American interests.

The Alien and Sedition Acts were the first to attempt to regulate immigration, and although they passed under the banner of national security, most historians agree the Acts were basically an attempt by President Adams to limit the number of voters who disagreed with his Federalist political party and who favored Thomas Jefferson as the next president. Regardless, Adams lost the presidency to Jefferson, and key parts of the Acts expired in 1800 or were repealed in 1802. The first legal attempt to limit immigration was ended, and the rest of the 1775 to 1840 period featured two events that created a great push for immigration in the following years — the Louisiana Purchase and the Industrial Revolution.

President Jefferson bought Louisiana from the French in 1803 (Napoleon needed the money). The colony covered most of the north-central area of what would become the enlarged United States, and its purchase practically doubled the size of the existing nation. The land would be distributed during the 1800s by a series of laws making acquisition of land in the region relatively simple. It became a magnet for immigrants who often had no hope of ever owning land in their country of origin. The land would also become a magnet for many Americans who felt "overcrowded" in the East as the population of the United States soared past seven million by 1810.

The Industrial Revolution originated in Great Britain and Western Europe. Driven by the development of an effective steam engine (which was initially used to pump water out of the ever deeper mines needed for coal mining), by James Watt in England in 1769, steam-powered products soon began to appear. The product with the most substantial impact in the United States in the early 19th century was the steam locomotive and the subsequent railroad system.

Introduction

Ironically, the first operational (although experimental) steam locomotive in the United States was built in 1825 at nearly the same time the Erie Canal, connecting New York City to Lake Erie and the Midwest, was opened. The Erie Canal was initially derided but it was a great success, and cities rushed to copy it. But the steam locomotive and the railroads would eventually replace all such canals. In 1830, the Baltimore and Ohio railroad began operation, notably replacing a planned canal that would have run from Baltimore to the Ohio River. This was a beginning that would ultimately find more miles of railroad track laid in the United States in the 1800s than anywhere else in the world.

But someone had to build those tracks and the many industrial companies they connected. The answer to the problem was the cheap labor of immigrants. Before 1840 the doors to immigration swung wide open. This started the largest influx of immigrants ever known into the United States in terms of the number of new immigrants who arrived compared to the number of residents already here. In the 1840s the number of immigrants would pass one million for the first time (it reached 1.7 million). From 1830 to 1930, about 38 million new immigrants arrived while the nation's population grew from 13 million to 123 million. The peak of 8.8 million occurred 1901–10, while the nation's population stood at 76 million as the century began.

1840 to 1924

While the period from 1840 to 1924 is often seen as the golden age of immigration in the United States, there were great differences between what happened on the East Coast (among immigrants primarily from Europe) and the West Coast (among immigrants primarily from Asia). However, over 80 percent of all immigrants to the United States in the 19th century were European. But by 1924, strong restrictions were placed on immigration from nearly all countries when the flood of immigrants was finally seen to be too much of a good thing.

In the 1840–1924 period, the Industrial Revolution essentially had a double effect on immigration to the United States. It produced a huge demand for cheap labor, especially after the Civil War ended in 1865, but in Europe it produced undesirable economic and social changes for many in what was a relatively crowded place where those doing menial labor could rarely hope for advancement. Hence, the United States was seen as a pillar of hope where much land was available, and the United States in turn was anxious for new immigrants to provide labor as industrialization steadily progressed through the century. Further, Ireland, which at the time had a very high population density, was stricken with a potato blight in the later 1840s, and because the potato was a key staple of the Irish diet, famine followed. What had been a steady flow of immigrants due to changes in the use and control of the land in Ireland became a flood by the 1850s. Immigration to the United States became a common solution to problems in countries where prior agricultural activities were greatly changed by the effects of the Industrial Revolution in Europe. The exodus of emigrants from Europe to the United States continued into the 20th century.

Between the 1840s and 1920s, by country of origin, there were about 6 million German immigrants, 4.75 million Italians, and 4.5 million Irish. The Irish predominated in the early 1850s, the Germans during much of the rest of the 1800s, and then the Italians in the late 1890s and into the early 1900s. Nearly every part of Europe contributed to the immigrant influx. But these European immigrants settled mostly in the Northeast or Midwest. On the West Coast, mostly Chinese or Japanese immigrants arrived in San Francisco, but the immigrants to the West Coast arrived in monthly totals of thousands rather than the hundreds of thousands arriving monthly in East Coast cities, overwhelmingly in New York.

The flood of immigrants arriving in the United States in the 1840–1924 period brought out a corresponding flood, so to speak, of anti-immigrant feeling, discrimination, and blatant racism. As the European immigrants included more and more Catholics, the heavily Protestant East reacted with animosity ranging up to and including riots. The early arriving Irish, especially those disembarking in Boston, were soon greeted with notices of "NINA," meaning "No Irish Need Apply." Real estate transactions included stipulations that the property in question could never be sold to anyone of Irish descent. But as is so often the case, later generations of Irish-Americans displayed great prejudice towards later groups of immigrants from other areas.

On the West Coast, anti-immigrant feeling towards the Chinese grew

Introduction

so strong that in 1882 Congress passed an act barring most Chinese from entering the United States at all. It is notable that this act was passed well after Chinese immigrants had completed the western section of the transcontinental railroad in 1869, seven years ahead of schedule and in only half the time allotted for its completion. The transcontinental railroad, running from the Mississippi River through the formidable Sierra Nevada mountains down to the West Coast at San Francisco, was the greatest engineering and construction feat of the century. It contributed much to the economic growth of the country with the great expansion of trade the new railroad links made possible.

It is symbolic that the Union Pacific Railroad, built westward from the Mississippi towards the West Coast employed over 10,000 men at its peak, the majority of which were much-maligned Irish-Americans. Similarly, the Central Pacific Railroad, hand-blasting and hand-digging 12 tunnels east through the Sierra Nevadas before it crested the summit and could race towards the Union Pacific coming west, also peaked at a workforce of over 10,000, of which 80 percent were Chinese immigrants. These same Chinese were soon to be barred from the United States as part of the "Yellow Peril" which was seen as a great threat to the United States by many. The greatest construction feat of the century was completed by immigrants who were suffering the effects of fierce discrimination by those already here.

The Chinese were an especially interesting case. They were originally considered too slight for such work, but the Central Pacific was desperate for labor. The Central Pacific suffered incredible turnover with its regular workforce because many workers, who had signed on to the railroad building task only to get a quick cash stake (and free transportation into the high Sierras), quit the railroad to go prospecting for what was left of the California gold rush and new silver stakes that were being found, especially in Nevada (relatively easily reached by a miner starting in the high Sierras of California). Besides, many of those familiar with the rugged Sierra Nevadas had no interest in the tedious and dangerous job of trying to build a railroad through and over them. The Central Pacific found the Chinese immigrants perfect for the task. They worked well in groups, cooked their own food (mainly boiled rice and tea), kept in good shape and had relatively few sick days. Many of the Chinese were not immigrants per se, but "sojourners" who had come to the United States to work and save enough cash to buy their own estates back in China ($450 was a typical goal) and live like kings in that desperately poor country.

Even while working with the great efficiency that enabled the transcontinental railroad to be built seven years ahead of schedule, it took five years from the official start of the "race" between east and west in 1862 for the Chinese immigrants to reach the summit of the Sierra Nevadas. Two years later in 1869, the east and west lines were connected in Utah, and the Chinese immigrants who did not head for a life of ease in China returned to the West Coast and became a great drag on the labor market there. A decade later the Chinese exclusion law was passed and stayed in effect until 1943.

A brief summary of the Chinese immigrant experience would read that foreign immigrants with a completely different language and culture than that in the United States arrived here and tended to band together; did vitally important work of a nature many resident Americans had little interest in; included some immigrants who only wanted to take money (or send it) back to their country of origin; and suffered great discrimination because they were "different" and were suspected of wanting to "take over." It's actually a story heard many times previously in the United States, but, more to the point, it's a story being heard today many decades later.

As the immigration flood swelled through the beginning of the 20th century (almost 19 million immigrants, half the total between 1830 and 1930, arrived between 1900 and 1930), concerns grew about the nearly unrestricted nature of the flow. The Immigration and Naturalization Service (INS) was created in 1891 to attempt to bring some order to the process. The INS opened the Ellis Island screening station in New York Harbor in 1892, and nearly 12 million immigrants, mostly in the early 1900s, were processed through this single facility. The first World War in 1914–1918 slowed the immigration process, and many Americans became suspicious about the patriotism of arriving immigrants. In the decade from 1915 through 1924, there was what would now be called a "witch hunt" for communists and anarchists. The attitude towards immigrants in the United States turned strongly negative.

There had been attempts in the first part of the 20th century to limit immigration. In 1907 the United States and Japan had signed a "Gentlemen's Agreement" in which Japan agreed not to issue passports to Japanese laborers seeking to enter the United States in exchange for a promise by the United States not to issue laws totally barring Japanese as had been the case with the Chinese. The fact that Japan was seen as a major power following its success in the 1904–1905 war with Russia while China was seen as a weak country played an important part in this agreement.

A major change in immigration law came with the Immigration Act of 1917. The law imposed a literacy test for all immigrants and established an Asiatic Barrier Zone, which barred immigrants from much of eastern Asia and many Pacific islands. All immigrants had to meet stricter personal, economic, and ideological standards. This law was simply a "warm-up" for the imposition of a quota system in 1921, where immigrants could only be admitted based on a measure of their country's immigrants that were already present in the United States, and the passing of Immigration Act of 1924. The 1924 Act imposed an even stricter quota system aimed at reducing those immigrants deemed to be undesirable, and the act barred practically all Asians, thus reneging on the Gentlemen's Agreement of 1907 with Japan. The Japanese were outraged, and the 1924 Act was yet another step in the many disagreements that led to war with Japan in 1941.

As the Chronology shows in detail, these acts of the early 20th century (and even before) were just a few of the multitude of immigration acts, including those that were liberal or restrictive, that have been enacted in the United States since the late 19th century to the present. Many of the acts have been based on inaccurate data or the misinterpretation of good data, not to mention miscalculations of how specific groups would react to the provisions of the new laws. For example, the Dillingham Commission, appointed in 1907 to study immigration, issued a 41-volume report in 1911 that gathered data to support its predetermined conclusion that recent immigrants from southern and eastern Europe were inferior to "old" immigrants who came before 1900. The Dillingham Commission "findings" were used as the basis for much of the restrictive laws that followed through 1924.

Historian and author Roger Daniels coined the phrase "BOMSAT" data for the type used in writing immigration laws based on poorly defined data. The term is an acronym for a "Bunch of Men Sitting Around a Table." Such data became especially prevalent in attempts to put a figure on the number of illegal immigrants in the later 20th century, but as nearly all things concerned with immigration do, its precedents go back many years.

The literacy test imposed by the immigration laws circa 1920 is an example of one of the many issues that have repeated themselves over the centuries and continue to do so today. Requiring immigrants to be literate (in their own language, not English) seemed to be a good idea when the issue was first raised in the 1890s, but no law could get passed over the objection of manufacturing and farming interests who wanted no interference with the flow of the cheap labor they needed in the factories and mines. In fact, many businessmen had noted that it was the more educated workers who were stirring up such "radical" issues as unionism, and these businessmen preferred their workers illiterate, obedient, and cheap.

The presence of groups who want to maintain their flow of cheap labor at all costs have either lobbied against what they see as too-strict immigration laws or simply supported illegal immigration from the days of the illegal trade in African slaves in the 1800s to the illegal immigrants of today. These immigrants perform the necessary "stoop labor" to grow the nation's fruits and vegetables and other agricultural products. Without the implicit or overt support of many businesses in the southwestern United States, illegal immigration would have been much less of a problem during the 20th century in the United States, and would be less of a problem today.

Further, all of the immigration acts of "yesterday," no matter how strict they appeared to be, contained a number of exceptions. As any good lawyer can tell you, the exceptions eventually are defined to cover far more immigrants than originally planned, and immigration goes on no matter what the original intent of the act. As the acts then become more liberalized, immigration soars beyond the level anticipated. It has happened throughout the centuries, and continues to do so today.

1925 to 1964

In spite of the intended severity of the 1917, 1921, and 1924 immigration acts, the 1924 act was not fully implemented until 1929. Total immigration for the 1921 through 1930 decade was 4.1 million, higher than the 1891–1900 decade, and all decades prior to 1880. However, as the effects of the 1924 Act were phased in, the average yearly rate of immigration for the years 1925 through 1930 fell by 50 percent to 300,000 per year from 600,000 per year for the years from 1921 through 1924. The full implementation of the 1924 act and the arrival of the Great Depression in the 1930s finally cut immigration in the 1930s to its lowest level since the 1830s, one century before.

Both presidents Hoover, early in the decade, and Roosevelt, inaugurated in March 1933, told the INS to focus on the parts of the immigration laws that barred immigrants who were felt to be likely to require public assistance. With rise of dictatorships in Europe, movement out of countries like Germany and Italy became difficult for any purpose, let alone immigration. Only 500,000 immigrants were admitted to the United States during the 1930s.

World War II put a further crimp in immigration in the 1940s, but the movement of displaced persons, refugees, and even war brides generated an increase after the war in the late 1940s before the next significant revision in the immigration laws came in 1952. The final number of immigrants came to 1.0 million in the 1940s, but by the end of the decade the immigrant rate per month was running at more than 200,000 — an equivalent of 2.4 million per year.

The Immigration and Naturalization Act of 1952, otherwise known as the McCarran-Walter Act, was meant to be another restrictive immigration act because it was passed in a time of anti-communism that amounted almost to hysteria. President Truman vetoed the law because he found it too restrictive towards countries he felt the United States should be more supportive of, but Congress overrode his veto in June of 1952. Lawmakers did not want to appear "soft on communism" with mid-term elections coming in the fall of 1952. However, the act actually removed the Asiatic Barrier Zone and otherwise expanded the number of nations from which immigrants could apply for admission to the United States, even if their quotas were limited. There were always exceptions to exploit, and as is usual in immigration law, others acts giving preference to certain groups followed the 1952 act. Immigration to the United States climbed again during 1951–1960 to 2.5 million as these exceptions to the 1952 bill were maximized. The stage was set for a massive liberalization of the immigration laws in 1965.

1965 to the Present

When Lyndon Johnson was elected president in his own right in 1964 with large Democratic majorities in both houses of Congress (partially as a sympathetic reaction to the assassination of President Kennedy in 1963), he was able to implement many goals of the Kennedy administration that Kennedy himself could not push through Congress because of his very narrow win in 1960. The most publicized of Johnson's actions were a large number of civil rights laws, but Johnson also created the most sweeping liberalization of immigration laws in the history of the United States up to that time. The amendments to the Immigration and Naturalization Act that passed in 1965 set the tone for immigration practice through 2005. Then great changes occurred in the period from December 2005 through 2007.

The 1965 Act abolished national-origin quotas and set yearly totals of 170,000 for Eastern Hemisphere immigrants and 120,000 for Western Hemisphere immigrants. Preferences were established for close relatives of American citizens, and there were no numerical limits on spouses, children and parents of citizens, as well as certain categories of "special" immigrants. The "exceptions" expanded as time went on, as has always been the case in immigration law since the beginning of the nation.

Immigration has constantly grown since the passage of the 1965 Act (and subsequent revisions), reaching 3.3 million in the 1960s, 4.5 million in the 1970s, 7.1 million in the 1980s, and 9.1 million in the 1990s. The latter number surpasses the prior record of 8.8 million between 1901 and 1910. However, because of the amnesty program begun in 1986, the later numbers include a substantial number of individuals who were already living in the United States as illegal immigrants.

Illegal immigration has soared along with the growing total of legal immigrants entering the United States. It has generated emotional responses covering a full range, from those who think it is destroying the United States and must be stopped in any way possible to those who offer aid to illegals on the basis that they are honorable people simply seeking to feed their families in the best way they can. The actual truth is, as always, somewhere in between. The data in the next paragraph puts the issue in numerical context.

Introduction

The number of immigrants who have legally entered the United States since the 1600s is now approaching 75 million. By late 2007 it was estimated that as many as 12 million illegal immigrants are also in the United States. As estimates of the latter type are almost by definition imprecise, such totals must be taken as BOMSAT data as previously noted (data generated by a Bunch of Men Sitting Around a Table). The images such data evoke of millions of persons pouring across our southern border are not quite accurate because it is further estimated that at least 40 percent of illegal immigrants (if not half) gained entrance by simply obtaining a legal visitor's visa and then remaining in the United States when the visa expired. Such a practice is very common as visitor's visas are easy to obtain, and there is almost no way to readily determine if the person obtaining the visa actually left when the visa expired. Further, illegal immigrants are often found in cargo ships and ordinary commercial airline flights entering the United States from abroad. Illegal immigration is a very complex issue. But even the most conservative estimate puts total legal and illegal immigration into the United States since the 1600s at well over 80 million.

Critics point out that the United States makes itself a very tempting target for illegal immigration. First, any child of an illegal immigrant who is born in the United States is automatically a citizen of the United States. Thus, the child is immediately eligible for certain benefits the parents may not be on their own, not to mention the possible future benefits of being a citizen of the United States. This circumstance dates back to the early days of the nation when new citizens were welcome to help increase the population. Efforts to change the law by requiring some sort of residency period before awarding citizenship have often been proposed but have never succeeded.

Next, the application of "equal protection under the law" concepts such as those found in the 14th Amendment, originally created to insure proper treatment of freed slaves in their home states after the Civil War, guarantees anyone physically present in the United States, even if they are here illegally, equal protection under the law. This includes a free public education and basically free healthcare via the use of emergency rooms, and even some welfare benefits. Further, the use of such benefits by illegal immigrants is often facilitated by local ordinances that forbid institutions from asking applicants about their immigration status. The reasons for this range from local politics to statutes in the immigration laws that are practically contradictory in stating that illegal immigration is undesirable but which in the same breath forbid individuals from determining the status of a suspected illegal immigrant.

Third, based on prior practice and statements of political leaders, there is always the hope for another round of amnesty. The sum of all these issues is that it appears to many migrants that the key is to somehow get within the borders of the United States and stay there as long as feasible. In most ways it is possible to live as a citizen of the United States and reap substantial financial rewards, while insuring that your children will probably have all the future benefits of life as a citizen of the United States.

Probably the single biggest incentive for illegal immigrants to cross the border between the southwestern United States and Mexico is the large number of United States residents who wish such traffic to continue. In addition to large agricultural companies who operate "factories in the field," and big housing manufacturers who employ large numbers of immigrants to work on their low-cost (to build) houses, there are many small firms putting new roofs on existing houses and doing other general repairs, and many individuals having their lawns and their children tended by low-wage illegal immigrants.

For those opposed to illegal immigration and its consequences, and as noted below the number grew substantially in 2006 and 2007, there is a "catch-22" in American law that prevents them from doing anything about it. First, any attempt to prevent illegal immigration by individuals is voided by the courts on the basis that only the Federal Government can regulate immigration (if and when they choose to do so). Next, when illegal immigrants appear in a community, citizens are required to treat them like any other citizen under the equal protection clause of the 14th amendment, even if they are here illegally. Courts have consistently ruled that the act of entering the country illegally does not strip illegal immigrants of their right to equal protection under the law. Only if they commit additional illegal acts (such as fraudulently acquiring a social security number in order to work illegally) can any action be taken against them. But this only happens if and when the proper authorities choose to enforce the law.

The really new thing that has arisen relative to immigration recently

Introduction

is that a critical mass of residents has grasped the difference between legal immigration and illegal immigration. The majority of Americans are in favor of legal immigration as shown by the continuing liberalization of immigration laws in general, and the fact that the number of legal immigrants admitted to the United States in the first decade of the 21st century is at its highest rate ever in the history of the United States (see Appendix 1 of this book).

Because of the generally favorable attitude toward immigration in the United States, immigration advocates have tried hard to blur the line between legal and illegal immigration, even while paying lip service to the sentiment that "something must be done about illegal immigration." But the events of December 2005 through the summer of 2007 showed that there has been a sea change in the attitude towards immigration in the United States. The nation now identifies illegal immigration as a separate issue and has turned firmly against it. In this sense the events of December 2005 through the summer of 2007 are the most important in the history of immigration in this country. Illegal immigration has now been identified as the most important immigration issue. Accordingly, considerable attention is given to this period in the Chronology that follows this Introduction.

The Great Illegal Immigration Attitude Change of 2007

Basically, there have been four distinct periods in the history of immigration into the United States, with each having a specific attitude towards immigration. The first time the enumeration of immigrants was required was 1820, and for the next 80 years the attitude towards immigration was primarily positive (as it had been before 1820).

However, by 1900 (and two decades before on the West Coast relative to the much smaller number of Asian immigrants there), the attitude towards immigration turned strongly negative for a number of reasons. This resulted in a series of restrictive laws being passed in 1917, 1921, and especially in 1924. This second period lasted from 1900 until 1965, when the immigration laws were drastically changed along the lines of civil rights issues, and the primary sources of immigration into the United States changed from Europe to Latin America and Asia. The 1924 laws had been chipped away by the events of World War II and the coming of the United Nations, but the landmark change came in 1965.

The third period lasted from 1965 until the terrorist attacks of 2001. It featured continually more liberal laws towards immigration, and the development of substantial illegal immigration into the United States, both by foot traffic over the southern border (about 60 percent of the total), and the simple expedient of overstaying a legally issued visa (about 40 percent of the total). Few serious attempts were made to prevent such illegal immigration, and the immigration law of 1986 finally granted amnesty to about three million illegal immigrants. The 1986 law promised to halt illegal immigration by making it a crime to hire illegal immigrants, but no honest attempt was made to enforce the law. All subsequent laws through 2000 further liberalized immigration laws on balance, and even made it easier for illegal immigrants to enter the country and receive benefits once here.

The fourth period started with the 2001 attacks, and immigration was newly looked upon as a security issue. The Patriot Act of 2001, the Homeland Security Act of 2002, and much discussion followed, but relatively few concrete steps were taken that substantially affected immigration. The favorable view of immigration in general continued, and the number of illegal immigrants soared to an estimated 12 million by 2007 (meaning each illegal immigrant given amnesty in 1986 had been replaced by four new illegal immigrants). However, individual citizens began to question the influx of and apparent support given to illegal immigrants even if Congress apparently did not. The first salvo in what would become a new battle over illegal immigration as opposed to legal immigration was fired by the Republican controlled House of Representatives in December 2005.

The House passed a bill applying harsh new penalties to illegal immigrants, including the stipulation that illegal immigration should be declared a felony and those supporting it should also be criminally charged. In the spring of 2006, the Senate declared the House bill much too harsh in many ways, and passed one of its own with its usual liberal positions. The House promptly rejected this bill. This was done against the background of large numbers of illegal immigrants demonstrating and declaring their

Introduction

"right" to enter the country illegally, which as it turned out angered many Americans.

The 2006 legislative session ended with a "compromise" to build fences along the Mexican border. The bill was a bit of a sham in that Democrats noted that there would not be enough funds to complete such a fence, and because the Democrats thought they would prevail in the 2006 fall elections (which they did), they would simply pass their "comprehensive" immigration bill in 2007 ("comprehensive" was the Democratic code word for amnesty) and what they did in 2006 would no longer be an issue.

But what happened in 2007 essentially gave the fourth immigration period from 2001 through 2007 (and after) the name of the "Period of Enforcement." A novel attempt was made in the beginning of 2007 to propose a "comprehensive" immigration bill in the Senate when a group of both Democratic and Republican Senators (sometimes jokingly called "the gang of 12"), together with two key members of President Bush's administration wrote a bill behind the scenes with trade-offs that would appeal to both sides (the "Grand Bargain"). The Republicans would be given security issues at the border including the controversial fence as well as a temporary worker program and changes in the way legal immigrants were selected favoring needed skills. The Democrats essentially would get their amnesty program.

But the bill failed, after seeming to be on the verge of victory, due partly to poor strategic decisions by the Democratic Senate leader to hurry the bill along, but mainly due to a surprising revolt by the nation's conservative voters who strongly attacked the notion of amnesty (by whatever name) for illegal immigrants. The government lies (the only applicable word) regarding the failure to enforce the laws accompanying the 1986 amnesty got center stage, and there was a sense of outrage that special inducements were needed by the government to enforce the laws already on the books.

The popular revolt killed the bill, and many politicians scrambled to at least appear to favor enforcement rather than amnesty. The upcoming 2008 elections seemed to require that an enforcement position would be the winning one. The Homeland Security Budget was amended to include money to install the border fence and many other security issues lifted from the failed

Senate bill regarding security and enforcement. New bills were introduced to strengthen other security issues. But not a word was heard about amnesty.

The Homeland Security Department got ready to issue instructions about how employers must reply to letters requiring clarification of social security numbers fraudulently acquired by illegal immigrants to illegally obtain employment. Such letters had been widely ignored in the past, and employers' complaints about complying and losing many workers confirmed that employers knew very well they had knowingly hired (and were still hiring) illegal immigrants in violation of existing law. The employers had blithely ignored the law on the phony basis that they were not "knowingly" violating it. Their two-decade illegal run was coming to a close and they were accordingly in a state of panic.

Thus, the legislative cycle of 2007 established a new attitude towards immigration in the United States. Illegal immigration was firmly identified as a separate immigration category, and one that was classified as being totally undesirable. Much effort is now underway to enforce the existing laws against it, and to further strengthen such laws.

There were many signs that this change in attitude was developing during 2006. Many communities, led most famously by Hazelton, Pennsylvania, started to write local ordinances against illegal immigrants. These were usually finally rebuffed by the courts, but the number of communities and states writing such legislation climbed into the hundreds during 2006 and into the thousands during 2007. The much-publicized Senate battle of 2007 served as a focal point around which the anti-illegal immigrant sentiments could coalesce.

The basic argument against illegal immigration is that it represents, especially for those simply walking into the country as they choose, people who have entered the country without screening of any sort and who can thus bring anything or anyone with them. In a world filled with terrorist attacks, this is a dangerous practice. But beyond this aspect, an illegal immigrant is a person who has ignored existing laws governing legal entry and has taken the law into his or her hands and "jumped the line." Many Americans find this process offensive, and the argument that many illegal immigrants are poverty stricken seems nearly irrelevant in a world filled with poverty-stricken people far beyond the capacity of the United States to accommodate them all.

Introduction

The change in attitude towards enforcement of the laws covering illegal immigrants will need some adjustment time. Suddenly preventing illegal immigrants from working could cause some economic disruptions. Further, no matter how effective the fence on the border with Mexico may turn out to be, it is still two years from completion. Additionally, there is still no effective plan to identify those illegal immigrants (estimated to be 40 percent of the total) who enter the United States with a valid visa and then stay in the United States when the visa expires. There will certainly be some legislation to address these issues, but it now seems certain such legislation will not be of the "let's pretend" nature that verbally disparages illegal immigration while associated actions encourage it. Those days appear over.

Future legal immigration into the United States can be expected to stay at its current level of about one million persons per year, by far the highest level in the world, or even to increase. There is little organized effective opposition to legal immigration, and the laws governing it are generally unchanged from the (highly liberalized) versions of 2000 and before. In addition, legal immigration plays a mostly unnoticed positive role in helping the United States escape the demographic population problems of many western democracies which raise questions about the ability of present generations to pay the social insurance costs of future generations. The world's overall rate of population growth has been declining for decades, and doomsday books aside, the question for most western countries is how to cope with declining population, not the runaway growth once commonly (and erroneously) predicted.

An additional upward bias towards legal immigration will come from the degree of success of the fight against illegal immigration. As noted, employers have been ignoring the laws against hiring illegal immigrants for decades. The sudden enforcement of those laws will mean additional workers will be needed for some time to come. Temporary worker programs have been somewhat "poisoned" by the attitude of non-enforcement of illegal immigrant laws in that many temporary workers stayed on illegally in the United States after their "temporary" terms were over. As one Senator stated during the debate over the failed "comprehensive" bill in June, he wanted to be sure "temporary" meant truly temporary. It is possible legal immigrant quotas could be increased to bring more skilled workers to the United States.

Introduction

The significance of what happened from December 2005 through the summer of 2007 relative to immigration laws can not be overstated. The border security project is going ahead, and experience with the San Diego "Gatekeeper" Program shows that it can be made to work. Adding that to an honest enforcement program that dries up the illegally provided jobs the illegal immigrants seek infers a slow but constant reduction of illegal immigrants in the future. The new age of illegal immigration enforcement will hopefully lead to a new and expanded age of legal immigration the entire country can fully embrace.

The Chronology

As described in the preceding Introduction, the first permanent settlement by English immigrants in the land that would become the United States was made at Jamestown, Virginia, in 1607. Further permanent settlements were made early in the 17th century, and immigration to the United States continued on a steady basis afterwards. There was a huge wave of immigrants in the 19th century, and the flow didn't reach its peak until the early 20th century. About 38 million immigrants were counted from the early 1800s through 1930.

The flow of immigrants paused during the Great Depression of the 1930s and the years of World War II in the 1940s, following restrictive legislation from 1917 through 1924. But after additional restrictive legislation in 1952 (that proved less restrictive than it first appeared to be), the rate of immigration resumed a steady upward trend in the 1950s. The great liberalization of the immigration laws in 1965 (and in other similar laws that followed) resulted in a sharp increase in total immigration in every decade afterwards. By the end of the 20th century, immigration for the decade from 1990–1999 topped the old records set in 1900 through 1909. The rate has increased further in the early 21st century, together with an estimated flow of illegal immigrants reaching an estimated total of 12 million by 2007.

Before the landmark legislation of 1965, about 43 million legal immigrants had come to the United States since 1600, most of them from Europe. At present, by the end of 2007, including illegal immigrants, almost another 43 million immigrants will have come to the United States since 1965, most of them from the Americas and Asia.

1607

This chronology shows the key events that occurred in the saga of immigration into the United States in the five centuries from the 1600s through the 1900s, and on into the beginning of the 21st century through most of 2007.

May 1607— The first permanent settlement of immigrants from England was made at a place called Jamestown on the James River in the state of Virginia. The settlers landed in three ships, and one of their leaders was Captain Christopher Newport, who was hired by the Virginia Company in London to transport colonists. The Jamestown settlers led others that followed (including those from a 1621 settlement named Newport News) in establishing a thriving business of growing tobacco for which there was a ready market in Europe.

September 1609— Henry Hudson, an English explorer seeking the Northwest Passage in the service of his Dutch employers, sailed up the Hudson River as far as Albany, New York. The Dutch eventually settled what is now New York City, and later absorbed other settlements in the area from the Swedes, but 65 years later in 1674 lost all of their settlements in America to the English as a result of constant wars between the Dutch and England. This gave the English control of immigration along the entire eastern coastline of America until the Revolutionary War that began hostilities in 1775.

Also during 1609, Samuel de Champlain explored the lake that now bears his name, and the Spanish established Santa Fe in what is now New Mexico. These places also ultimately became part of the United States.

August 1619— The Dutch brought the first black laborers to Jamestown, Virginia. There is disagreement among reference sources as to whether these blacks were brought as indentured servants (workers who traded several years of labor for eventual freedom) or brought as slaves. Whatever the status of the 1619 group, slavery was legally recognized in the area by 1650 because cheap labor was needed to grow tobacco and other crops which were very labor intensive. Blacks from Africa were brought in the following years as unwilling "immigrants" until slaves made up twenty percent of the population of the United States by 1775.

December 26, 1620— A total of 103 Pilgrim separatists arrive at Plymouth Rock in Massachusetts after a journey of over three months from Plymouth, England on a ship named the *Mayflower*. This was the beginning of permanent immigrant settlements in New England. Over 20,000 so-called Puritans arrived from England in the next twenty years, with the establishment of the city of Boston occurring in 1630. This was a much larger number of settlers than elsewhere in the colonies, but the flow ended abruptly for a while in 1642 when a civil war broke out in England and additional potential emigrants waited to see if more favorable circumstances in their view might evolve in England.

1634— The state of Maryland was founded as a Catholic colony under a charter given to Lord Baltimore. An Act granting religious tolerance to all settlers was declared in 1649.

1654— The first sizable group of Jewish immigrants to America arrived at New Amsterdam (which became New York ten years later).

1660— Believing that, as taught by the doctrine of mercantilism, the wealth of a nation was dependent on its population, King Charles II took steps to discourage emigration from England by the general public. The reduced flow from England essentially resulted in increased diversity in the American colonies as they tried to gain population by looking to other sources such as continental Europe, Africa, and the West Indies.

Also in 1660, on December 1, the British Parliament passed the first Navigation Act, which despite its name, was intended to regulate the commerce of its colonies in a way that was favorable to British needs. Discouraging emigration and beginning the Navigation Acts were steps that began to fester in the American colonies and lead ultimately to war with England a century later.

April 1670— The city of Charles Town (Charleston), South Carolina, was established as the Carolina Territory was settled by a mix of about 100 English men and women who sailed from London with the mission to establish Charleston. Aid was received from a number of small planters who wished to escape the overcrowded Island of Barbados in the West

Indies. In 1680 they were joined by a group of French Huguenots. Those from Barbados were familiar with the system of using black slaves from Africa, and, by 1700, about half of the population of 7,000 of the South Carolina settlement consisted of slaves.

1681— William Penn, who had been given land by King Charles II for Penn's "holy experiment," founded Pennsylvania as a refuge for people of different nationalities and religions to live together in freedom. Penn's primary target were the Quakers of which he was a member, but he opened Pennsylvania ("Penn's Woods") to a wide range of immigrants, many of whom were attracted by Penn's very liberal policies on the eventual ownership of land in his newly established State.

April 23, 1683— William Penn signed a treaty with the Delaware Indians and made payment for Pennsylvania lands. During the year the first sizeable contingent of German immigrants came to America and settled near Philadelphia. Led initially by the Mennonites, many German sects followed, attracted in equal parts by religious freedom and the relative ease of eventually obtaining land in Pennsylvania. Until the end of the 19th century, Germany would be the leading country of origin for immigrants coming to the United States, and as late as 1920 would rank first as the leading country of origin for the highest percentage of persons of foreign-born origin in the United States (Germany would rank second as late as 1980).

1685— The growth of religious intolerance in France, capped by the revocation of the Edict of Nantes, resulted in a surge in the emigration of French Huguenots to America. Although their number was not especially large, they had a strong influence on the colonies they arrived in as immigrants because the Huguenots had an unusually high proportion of merchants, professional men, and craftsmen among their ranks. The Huguenots tended to settle in established towns like Charlestown, Philadelphia, New York, and Boston, where they achieved considerable political and commercial influence by the time of the Revolutionary War in 1775.

1697— The monopoly of the Royal African Company was ended resulting in an expanded slave trade generally. The infamous triangle between the colonies in the northern mainland of America, the "sugar islands" of the West Indies, and the Guinea coast of Africa was very profitable to ship merchants, and the number of slaves arriving in the colonies grew steadily, especially in the southern colonies. As noted, slaves made up one-fifth of the population of the colonies by the time the Revolutionary War hostilities began in 1775.

1707 — When England and Scotland agreed on an "Act of Union," Scotland was no longer a foreign country in the eyes of England, and more opportunities opened for Scots to emigrate to America in spite of the general discouragement towards emigration within England itself.

1709 — A mass exodus from the German Palatine (later known as the Rhineland) began, and many German immigrants headed for existing German settlements in Pennsylvania. The Germans would make a large proportion of all future immigrants to the United States as well as Pennsylvania in the years to come (see entry for April 23, 1683), resulting in a Nativist diatribe against them by none other than Benjamin Franklin in the 1750s. Germans would amount to one-third of the population of Pennsylvania at the time.

1717 — The British Parliament authorized the transportation of criminal felons to the American colonies. Previously petty thieves had served as indentured servants in the colonies, but now even criminals of a more serious nature were "dumped" in America, being seen as undesirables by the British even in light of the general discouragement against emigration.

1718 — In this year the British Parliament prohibited the emigration of skilled artisans as the Scotch-Irish begin to emigrate to the United States in large numbers. It was estimated as many as 250,000 Scotch-Irish came to America in the next half-century before hostilities began in the Revolutionary War. The prime reason for their departure to America was the termination of land leases on favorable terms that had been granted 30 years before to attract the Scotch to settle in Ireland. This became a constant irritant in Ireland over the years, and Scotch-Irish immigration to the colonies remained high leading up to the Irish famines of circa 1850 that sent nearly the entire island of Ireland into the mode of thinking about emigrating to the United States. Over four million would do so in the next 75 years.

1720—The trade in so-called Redemptioners became systemized in the American colonies. Whereas an indentured servant essentially signed up for a certain number of years of labor in the colonies before immigrating there, a Redemptioner sailed to the colonies as a free person like a regular colonist. However, upon arrival the Redemptioner was required to pay for transportation, and if unable to pay, as many were, the Redemptioner had to work in the colonies to pay the transportation debt.

Redemptioners were often from Germany while indentured servants were often from England and Ireland. The systemization of Redemptioners meant that Dutch merchants and ship owners started to recruit candidates in Germany and transports them to Amsterdam and Rotterdam for eventual shipment to the colonies. Abuses were common, but many poor Germans used the system to emigrate to America.

1727—The Pennsylvania Assembly, sharing the concern of its citizens that the large influx of Germans into the state might led to Germans trying to organize a separate German colony, decided to require incoming Germans to take an oath of allegiance to the king and an oath of fidelity to the proprietors of the state and the provincial Constitution.

1732—Confirming the perceived high percentage of Germans among non–English immigrants prior to the Revolutionary War (the Scotch-Irish were actually just as numerous), the first German language newspaper in America, the *Philadelphische Zeitung* was published during this year.

1775—The British Government suspended all immigration to its American colonies upon the outbreak of hostilities in Massachusetts in what would become the Revolutionary War. At the time, there were about 2.5 million people in the American colonies compared to nearly eight million in Great Britain. But even though the colonies would be fighting on their home ground, the disparity in population was even greater than it looked at first glance.

About 22 percent of the population of the colonies (more than 500,000 people) was black African slaves. There were approximately 250,000 Scots-Irish and 200,000 Germans among the rest of the white population of less than two million. However, both Spain and especially France offered aid to the colonial cause. Immigration from Europe to the colonies continued during the war even as that from England ceased.

September 3, 1783— Great Britain and the United States signed a peace treaty in Paris formally ending the Revolutionary War and recognizing the independence of the United States. The decisive battle had taken place near Williamsburg, Virginia, almost exactly two years earlier when a combined United States–French force defeated General Cornwallis of Great Britain. Immigration to the United States began slowly increasing again once the British were defeated even though a formal peace treaty had not yet been signed.

In the meantime, during 1783, the Massachusetts Supreme Court declared slavery to be illegal in that state. This had very little effect on the slave trade as the number of slaves in New England was very small (90 percent of all slaves in the United States were in the south below the Mason-Dixon line), but it gave impetus to the movement to ban the slave trade and the importation of new slaves throughout the United States.

July 13, 1787— The Continental Congress adopted the Northwest Ordinance. The ordinance covered the territory north of the Ohio River and west of New York. The ordinance gave rules for statehood, guaranteed support for schools and freedom of religion, and outlawed slavery in the new territory. The ordinance became very important to future immigrants, as it was essentially the first step in selling off the one great resource of the new country — land — as a way of paying war debts. Terms for acquiring the new land were quite reasonable and thus very attractive to immigrants who had no hope of ever owning land in their countries of origin.

The area covered by the Ordinance was basically the same as the area known as the "Ohio Territory," which marked the wild frontier of the country in revolutionary and even pre–Revolutionary times. As late as 1794, General "Mad" Anthony Wayne would be defeating Indian tribes along a string of forts in the area and even checking the meddling of the

British who were still stinging from their unexpected defeat in the Revolutionary War. One of the reasons for offering the land to all comers was to establish settlements in the area to serve as a buffer against further incursions by Indian forces and meddling foreign governments.

June 21, 1788— The Constitution of the United States became official after the required minimum of nine states ratified it (New Hampshire put it over the top after Delaware started the process in December of the previous year). The first Congress declared it in effect on March 4, 1789 after Washington's election as President.

One part of the Constitution encouraged immigration to the new country (as had the Declaration of Independence in 1776), but in spite of these welcoming words and the need for new immigrants to provide labor and population growth, local tensions still occurred between new immigrants and established citizens. It was a process that had been ongoing since the early 1600s and would continue for more than two centuries into the future.

One notable aspect of the Constitution was that it provided for the end of the international slave trade in twenty years (which would be in 1807 counting from the date of the submission of the Constitution for ratification). But there was no limitation placed on the process of slavery as presently conducted within the borders on the United States. The international slave trade would in fact became illegal in the United States in 1807, but one result would be the first appearance of "illegal immigrants" in the United States, as many southern plantation owners would pay for the illegal importation of black slaves into the United States to maintain their cheap labor base. Only the end of the Civil War in 1865 would end the process.

April 30, 1789— George Washington was inaugurated as the first president of the United States, as all of the basic operating functions of the new government were put into place during the year of 1789. Washington, as was typical of Virginia estate owners of his time, owned slaves and had a number of indentured servants to run his agricultural operations based at Mount Vernon, Virginia.

Washington supported attempts to keep the indentured servant trade alive as well as the immigration of skilled artisans, both of which the British were attempting to stop with a variety of laws during the period. Many people in the United States saw the immigration of skilled indentured servants and skilled artisans as necessary for the establishment of a manufacturing capability in the United States. The British, who saw their defeat by a "rag tag" continental army in the Revolutionary War as a fluke, were not inclined to be of any help in this area, and they ignored many other aspects of the 1783 peace treaty as well. A treaty would be signed in 1794 between the United States and Britain to attempt to address these issues, but it would take the War of 1812 to obtain resolutions of most problems.

March 26, 1790—A Naturalization Act was passed by the Congress of the United States requiring a residency period of two years in the United States and one year in the state of residency before an immigrant could apply to be a citizen of the United States. The act applied only to aliens who were "free white persons" of "good moral character." The racial aspect of this act would only be modified in the 1860s after the Civil War to include the freed slaves and thus persons of African-American descent. It would be used in future immigration laws to bar the immigration of persons who were not "eligible for citizenship," i.e., non-whites such as Asians. The racial aspect of the act would finally be eliminated by the McCarran-Walter Act of 1952 (see entry for June 27, 1952).

There was considerable debate in Congress over this issue between those who felt the United States should offer asylum to the world as a place founded on absolute freedom for all, and those who felt many immigrants were undesirable and even a threat to the security of the United States. The two-year period was a victory for those urging a liberal approach, but the debate went on after the Act was passed (and goes on in a similar vein even today).

For eligible persons, becoming a citizen was a very simple process in those days. A "Petition for Naturalization" was filed with any convenient court having jurisdiction over the petitioner's residence. Upon being satisfied with the applicant's good moral character, the court would administer an oath of allegiance to the Constitution of the United States. The court clerk's recording of the process would make the applicant a citizen. The act further conferred citizenship upon the children of citizens even if they were born outside the borders of the United States.

1791

1791 — A revolt of blacks broke out on the French island of Santa Domingo. The entire white population fled during the next two years, and ten or twenty thousand of them eventually found refuge in the United States (as had many fleeing the guillotine and the French Revolution of 1789). Most of the Santa Dominicans arrived destitute, but sympathetic Americans raised funds to help them by public subscription, and Congress voted $15,000 in 1794 for their relief. This started a typical reaction in Congress over the next two centuries of providing funds for immigrants fleeing their native land due to wars, rebellions, adverse changes in government, or natural disasters and so forth.

1793 — Eli Whitney invented the cotton gin. This was just part of his inventive genius which greatly helped an infant American manufacturing capability to grow with his invention of "replaceable parts," but from an immigration standpoint, the cotton gin inadvertently increased the importation of black slaves to the United States. High costs had been causing a slowdown in the cotton industry in the south, but the efficiency of the cotton gin increased the profitability of the cotton industry, and the demand for black slaves increased.

January 29, 1795 — The Naturalization Act of 1790 (see entry for June 1798) was amended to extend the waiting period for immigrants before applying for citizenship from two to five years in the United States and from one to two years in the state of residence. In addition, immigrants were required to renounce any titles of nobility they might hold from their country of origin. The Act still applied only to "free white persons."

Immigration had become a political issue. The Federalists, the party of President Washington and Vice-President John Adams, saw the many "radicals" among immigrants as pursuing the downfall of the new government of the United States, while Jefferson and his fellow Republicans liked the "progressive" ideas of such immigrants but wanted nothing to do with what they saw as hangovers from royalty. Hence the two issues of a longer waiting period and the renouncement of prior titles had something for each party.

The naturalization process was also made more complicated. Now a petitioner had to make a Declaration of Intention at their local court at least three years prior to filing for final naturalization. Then petitioners were notified that in addition to swearing allegiance to the Constitution of the United States, they would have to renounce allegiance to their former sovereign at the final step in the naturalization process.

June 1798—With John Adams as president (elected over Thomas Jefferson in a close contest in 1796), Congress passed four laws known collectively as the Alien and Sedition Acts. The Acts were passed at the urging of Adams on the basis of improved security for the new nation, but most historians since have argued their prime purpose was to silence those in political opposition to Adams, and to reduce the number of immigrants who could vote, presumably not in favor of Adams in the next election.

One of the Acts, a revised Naturalization Act, lengthened the years of residency needed to apply for citizenship from five years to fourteen (and from the two years originally set in 1790). The required for notification of intent was increased from three years to five years. During the debate there were efforts to limit citizens to those born in the United States. There were two Alien Acts (the Alien Enemies Act and the Aliens Friends Act) permitting the President arbitrary powers to seize and expel resident aliens suspected of being engaged in subversive activities. Finally, there was the Sedition Act aimed at silencing foreign-born writers and journalists who criticized the government.

The part of the Naturalization Act requiring 14 years of residence was set back to 5 years in 1802 (individual states had essentially ignored it anyhow), and the Alien and Sedition Acts expired in 1800. So their effects were short-lived, but they marked the first really serious effort to control immigration into the United States. The political intentions also misfired as Jefferson won the presidency in 1801 (by a vote in the House after a tie with Aaron Burr in the electoral vote in 1800), and Jefferson continued to be a prime supporter of immigration.

December 20, 1803—The United States took title to the Louisiana Purchase in a transaction negotiated between President Jefferson and Napoleon of France. The addition of the Louisiana Territory effectively doubled the size of the United States, extending the nation's northern border from the Atlantic Ocean to the Pacific Ocean in one stroke. More than ever it made the United States a preferred destination for those immigrants seeking land, and it gave the United States an added incentive to encourage immigration as a way to settle the huge new land area it had just acquired.

Other events would lead to an unprecedented wave of immigration to the United States in the 19th century: by the time of the Louisiana Purchase the new nation had essentially come to terms with the phenomena of immigration. All who wanted to come were welcome, but no special incentives would be offered to do so. For the rest of the century immigration would be handled in a business-like manner, and it would become, in fact, mainly a matter of doing business and a way of meeting the needs of the country.

1808—The banning of the United States in the international slave trade that had been written into the Constitution in 1787 was in effect for its first full year in 1808. However, in the south, the main effect was to create the nation's first sizeable group of "illegal immigrants." It is estimated that between 50,000 and 250,000 slaves were illegally imported into the United States between 1808 and 1860 before the Civil War began in 1861.

June 18, 1812—The War of 1812 began against Britain when Congress unknowingly declared war two days after the British blockade of France, one of the immediate causes of the war, had been lifted. However, there were many other prime complaints against Britain, which never had really accepted its defeat in the Revolutionary War. This time the two nations were more nearly equal in population (with Britain near 10 million and the United States near 8 million), and this time the United States had a formidable Navy thanks mainly to the efforts of John Adams, who had pressed for "walls of wood" while he was both president and vice-president in the 1790s.

Also, a decade earlier, the United States had won a war with Tripoli caused by the refusal of the United States to pay tribute to the Arabs to prevent raids against American shipping ("millions for defense but not a penny for tribute" was the cry of one American politician). The United States was no longer just a poor cousin among the nations of the world, and this would help to make it an irresistible target in the eyes of immigrants in the years to follow.

Following a series of naval victories by the United States during the war, a peace treaty was signed at Ghent, Belgium, on December 24, 1814, to end the War of 1812 only 30 months after it began. Unfortunately for the British, they suffered one of their most stinging defeats of the war in the Battle of New Orleans on January 8, 1815, with both sides unaware a peace treat had been signed two weeks earlier. The British suffered more than 2,000 causalities in a force of 5,300 men while the United States suffered only 71.

Although the War of 1812 was really only a footnote in the military history of the United States, and in many ways was basically a stand-off, some historians think it played a significant role in the historical surge of immigration to the United States that took place in the 1800s following 1815. First of all, the war caused the British to cease interfering with the flow of immigrants to America, including stopping ships bound for America to "impress" its inhabitants (essentially kidnap potential immigrants for service in the British navy). The British also ceased meddling with Indian tribes to stir up hostilities with the United States along its prior western border in the Ohio Territories, even though some of these issues took several more years to fully resolve.

Spain was sufficiently impressed with the results of the war to cede Florida to the United States at the beginning of 1819. Spain granted independence to Mexico two years later, and Texas broke away in 1836 and joined the United States in 1845. The part of the southwestern United States previously held by Mexico/Spain inevitably was brought into the United States before 1850 by a series of "treaties" that were unfavorable to Mexico.

The consequences of the War of 1812 effectively included the Monroe Doctrine of 1823, which told all European countries to recognize the United States as being predominant of all of the Americas. These countries accepted it because no one was anxious by then to take on the United States in disputing it.

In this way, the United States became the beacon of hope for immigrants all over the world. The United States had huge amounts of land to offer, and it was obvious that no foreign country was going to intervene in a way that would dash the hopes of the immigrants in any respect. The huge immigrant influx of about 38 million people that followed in the more than a century after the War of 1812 was triggered by many events, but the emergence on the United States as an unquestioned power in the world was one of the first steps.

December 1816— A group named the American Colonization Society was formed in Washington, D.C., with the intention of performing a sort of reverse immigration by transporting free blacks to Africa. Paul Cuffe, a black who had been born free on an island off Massachusetts in 1759, had founded a shipping line and formed a colony in Sierra Leone in Africa in 1811. He hoped to start an exodus of free blacks to Sierra Leone, but the War of 1812 intervened, and by the time he transported 38 free blacks to Sierra Leone in 1816, conditions had changed there and he was not greeted warmly by the unstable government. He was convinced to try to help the newly formed American Colonization Society in its goals, but Cuffe's health failed soon after and he died in 1817.

The America Colonization Society (full name The Society for the Colonization of Free People of Color of America) was a hybrid organization of groups who had different motives for joining together to reach a common goal which involved removing blacks from America. There were Southern Plantation owners who were wary of free blacks (about 200,000 or ten percent of the then two million blacks in the United States population) because the plantation owners feared the free blacks would lead a slave revolt (black slaves were still being imported into the south illegally). There were Northerners who feared an influx of blacks would hurt economic opportunities for indigent whites, and there were various moralists who wanted freedom for slaves and their descendents. All groups felt there was no real hope of integrating blacks into American society because of color discrimination.

The common solution was felt to be the emigration of blacks to their own independent state in Africa, and for the next three years they attempted to raise money for that goal. They finally obtained $100,000 from Congress in 1819, and that put them over the top in their attempt to arrange transportation to Africa. In February of 1820, their first ship, the Elizabeth, with 86 free blacks aboard sailed for Sierra Leone. These settlers, along with 2,638 others from subsequent trips, plus others from an arrangement with the United States government to accept freed blacks captured from illegal slave ships, eventually formed the independent state of Liberia which declared its independence in 1847.

1819— The American steamship *Savannah*, which was partly powered by steam as well as the conventional sails, crossed the Atlantic from Savannah, Georgia, to Liverpool, England, in just 29 days. Fully sail-powered crossings could easily take a few months at that time depending on wind and weather. It would take some years to develop fleets of steam-powered ships, but this semi-experimental crossing marked the beginning of yet another aid to the immigration tide that would flow to the United States during the rest of the 1800s and into the early decades of the 20th century.

Also, in 1819, Congress passed an act requiring shipmasters to deliver a manifest listing all aliens transported on their ships for immigration to the United States. The Secretary of State was required to report annually to Congress on the number of immigrants admitted to the United States. This act not only brought more order to the immigration process, but also became a boon to historians writing about the history of immigration.

1825— The year 1825 was a turning point in the perceived need for immigrant labor in the United States. The year can be taken as the time the Industrial Revolution, starting with the development of the steam engine in England in 1769, came to full flower in the United States.

The Erie Canal, connecting the Great Lakes to New York Harbor via upstate New York at Buffalo to Albany and the Hudson River to New York City, opened with the first boat leaving Buffalo on October 26th and arriving in New York City on November 4. The canal was a great success, and although skeptics originally derided it, they raced to copy it as soon as its success was obvious. Much of the labor to dig the canal was provided by Irish immigrants, and if there were going to be more canals, there would have to be more immigrants.

But as successful as the canal was, a more significant event took place in the same year of 1825. John Stevens, of Hoboken, New Jersey, built and operated the first experimental steam locomotive in the United States. Eventually the steam locomotive and the railroad tracks on which it would run would replace the Erie Canal and all its descendents. Starting in 1828, the famous Baltimore and Ohio Railroad would be operational by 1830 (notably having replaced a planned canal that would have run from Baltimore to the Ohio River near Pittsburgh), and the United States was on its way to laying more miles of railroad track than anyone else in the world.

However, someone would have to build all those miles of railroad track, and that "someone" would turn out to be more immigrants. Fortuitously for the United States, the Industrial Revolution in Europe was causing social and economic changes that were making many people consider leaving their homeland, and as they learned more about the powerful and prosperous United States, full of jobs and available land, it quickly became their target of choice. The stage was set for an immigration tide that would be greater than any other in history to that point. And in terms of new arrivals to a country compared to the number of persons already there, it would become an immigration tide that would never be topped.

The United States began to collect immigration statistics in 1820. In the decade of the 1820s, 129,000 immigrants arrived, with 1825 marking a turning point as described above. In the decade of the 1830s, the number soared to 0.6 million. In the decade of the 1840s, the number of immigrants passed one million for the first time, reaching a total of 1.4 million. After that, the number of immigrants would exceed two million in every decade until the Great Depression of the 1930s.

To put the numbers in perspective, the number of immigrants who arrived between 1815 (after the end of the War of 1812) and 1860, the year before the Civil War began, was about five million. This number approximately equaled the total population of the United States in 1800. And this was just the beginning of the wave of immigrants to come. In the ten years from 1845 through 1854 inclusively, three million immigrants would arrive in a country of only about 30 million people. This still represents the greatest inflow of immigrants in proportion to the existing population the United States has ever known.

1840— Steadily increasing trade by ship between Europe and the United States in this era had a dramatic effect on immigration from Europe to the United States. This was because the greater ship traffic meant a greater number of established routes and schedules to and from the United States, and more ships from Europe were looking for a profitable cargo on the westward leg of their journey from Europe to the United States. They picked up lumber, cotton, and tobacco in the United States, and these bulky products filled the eastbound ships. But much space was available on the westbound ships carrying manufactured products from Europe. The increasing tide of immigrants to the United States meant a much lower fare per person, which in turn meant more persons responding to the lower fares.

As early as 1820, more than a thousand ships were utilized in carrying newly expensive timber from North America (including Canada) to the British Isles. By 1840 that number had more than doubled. At the same time, the number of ships annually carrying cotton to Liverpool had risen from about 300 in 1820 to more than a thousand by 1840. Similar increases occurred in traffic to continental Europe. Since it was a relatively simple matter to build temporary bunks in the hold of a freighter, ships carrying freight eastbound were quickly converted to "passenger" ships westbound. "Passenger agents" made their appearance about this time, and ship traffic in the human cargo of immigrants grew quickly.

The potential number of immigrants had also been growing rapidly in the meantime. In the mid–1820s Britain repealed its restrictions on emigration, mostly to encourage poor Irish peasants to go to the United States rather coming to Britain and developing an even bigger underclass. It was a time of great population growth in Europe, and other countries began to relax emigration restrictions as well with a view towards reducing paupers in their countries. Later, after the German revolution of 1848, Germany relaxed its restrictions as well to reduce the number of potential trouble makers, which led to an exodus from Germany, although most of the emigrants were not involved in revolutionary activities per se but simply took advantage of the reduced restrictions.

Thus, the combination of more potential emigrants and more readily available (and cheaper) transportation led to an increased flow of immigrants into the United States from 1820 through 1840. Then the Irish famine of the late 1840s turned a flow measured in the tens and 50s of thousands into a flood measured in the multiple hundreds of thousands (see entries for 1847 and 1851).

May 1, 1841— Internal migration in the United States was beginning to take place over long distances as waves of new immigrants came ashore on the East Coast. The first emigrant wagon train (with a total of 41 persons) left Independence, Missouri, for California on this date. It arrived a little over 6 months later on November 4, taking roughly twice as long as the slowest immigrant ship traveling across the Atlantic Ocean to the United States. But the internal emigrants and the foreign immigrants were driven by the same desire for a better life.

1847— This year marked the middle of a series of potato blights in Ireland. The tiny island was densely populated and had been overcrowded for some time, and onerous land rents had previously sent Irish immigrants to the United States in a steady flow for several decades, especially after the British relaxed some immigration restrictions after the War of 1812 (see entry for June 18, 1812). But the potato blight and resulting famine turned the steady flow into a flood. About 1.5 million people left Ireland for the United States in the decade after 1847. By 1850 the residents of New York were 26 percent Irish. About 2.8 million in total left Ireland between 1820 and 1880, outnumbering all immigrants except those from Germany in that period. The United States received 4.5 million Irish immigrants by 1930, exceeding all but Germans (6 million) and Italians (4.75 million) in the first 150 years of the existence of the new nation.

The population of Ireland was a dense 8.3 million in 1846, just before the failure of the potato harvest. But the population fell to 5.8 million by 1861, as over one million people died of starvation beyond the 1.5 million that emigrated to the United States. The population of Ireland fell to 4.5 million by the turn of the century in 1901, a number almost exactly equal to the number of Irish immigrants who had come to the United States since the failure of the potato harvest in 1847. It became literally true that the number of Irish who had emigrated to the United States (even ignoring the natural increase of the Irish in the United States) outnumbered the total population of the "home" country just before Ireland broke with Britain and became a separate Republic in 1922. There were more "home-born" Irish in the United States than in Ireland. No other country had such an incredible ratio. The Germans and Italians, the only immigrants to outnumber the Irish, came from countries having 1900 populations of 56 million and 32 million respectively.

February 2, 1848— The Treaty of Guadalupe Hidalgo was signed ending the Mexican War. The War had begun in May of 1846 when United States troops seized land in dispute between Texas (admitted to the Union five months before) and Mexico. The United States easily won the war, and dictated the terms of the treaty. Mexico ceded all of its remaining claims to Texas (which had won its independence from Mexico in 1836), and also ceded California and its other territory in the southwestern United States. This treaty extended citizenship to approximately 80,000 Mexicans living in Texas, California, and the American southwest.

This treat also completed the map of the continental United States essentially as we know it today, and it opened vast additional acreage to both international immigrants and those citizens already here who felt "crowded" in the east. The internal emigration made additional room for the international immigrant tide flowing primarily into the eastern United States. When gold was discovered in California on January 24, 1848, just before the peace treaty with Mexico was being signed, the general westward movement of people in the United States was set nearly permanently in motion.

The announcement of the discovery of gold in California attracted people from all over the world as well as from the United States. About 80,000 prospectors emigrated to California in 1849 (including Chinese immigrants who would total about 20,000 by 1851). However, a total of almost 300,000 immigrants came to the United States in 1849. Gold was only one of the many items attracting immigrants to the United States. The total increased steadily to a then record peak of almost 428,000 in 1854, before declining again as the Civil War approached in 1861.

July 1848— A converted Maine whaler, named the *Wiscasset*, left the port of Glasgow, Scotland, carrying a cargo of immigrants headed for the United States. Such cargoes had become very profitable to shipping interests, and sailing ships of every variety were being pressed into service. A company called Taylor and Merrill in New York, who had started their own transatlantic line in 1842, and were adding additional ships to draw additional profits from the immigrant trade, owned the *Wiscasset*.

Included on the ship was the Carnegie family, which was sailing for the United States because the father of the Carnegie family had failed in

1849

his weaving business and relatives had established prior residence in Pittsburgh, Pennsylvania. The Carnegies had borrowed money from a friend, and planned to live with their relatives in Pittsburgh until they could get established. Their older son was four months shy of his thirteenth birthday, but stated his age as fifteen. It was common for emigrants coming to the United States to claim age levels that were more likely to get them jobs when they arrived. Carnegie's father Will claimed to be forty rather than his actual age of forty-four, because younger men were more likely to get jobs. His mother Mag, who was thirty-eight, claimed to be thirty-four for the same reason.

The older son was known as Andra, but his given name was Andrew, and as Andrew Carnegie, he became one of the richest men in the world, starting from zero when he arrived in the United States. Twenty years later, when Andrew Carnegie was already a millionaire at the tender age of thirty-three, he took a trip to Europe to sell bonds for railroads and railroad bridges. He was a regular traveler by that time, and his trip to Europe would take only five days on the fastest ship then available. But in 1848, the trip from Europe on the *Wiscasset* took five weeks instead of five days, and this was unusually fast for the ships traveling across the Atlantic in 1848. Few immigrants had success at the level enjoyed by the hardworking Andrew Carnegie, but all of them had to spend anywhere from five to seven weeks on the ocean passage in ships that were not originally built for passengers and were not especially comfortable.

1849— The sudden rise in immigration caused the states of New York and Massachusetts, where most immigrants were arriving, to levy taxes and create other restrictions on immigration. These "Passenger Cases" were settled this year by a Supreme Court ruling. The state laws were struck down as being unconstitutional. The Court stated that although the Constitution said nothing about immigration directly, it clearly was "foreign commerce" of the type the Constitution explicitly reserved to the control of Congress. Thus, only Congress could regulate immigration.

1850— For the first time, the United States Census recorded the "nativity" of citizens, i.e., whether they were born inside or outside the United States.

1851— The year of 1851 marked the end of a frantic six year period from 1846 through 1851 when Irish peasants flooded the north Atlantic to escape the Irish Famine by fleeing to the United States (see entry for 1847). The process went on throughout the rest of the 1800s, but the 1846–51 period marked a peak. About 5,000 ships carrying Irish emigrants crossed the Atlantic in this period, and they varied greatly in size, comfort, and safety — or the lack thereof.

Many of the ships originated from the British port of Liverpool, to which the Irish were ferried from Ireland. Liverpool had a long history of profitable participation in the slave trade, going from Europe to West Africa with limber and other provisions, bringing slaves from Africa to the United States, and returning to Liverpool with cotton, tobacco, and wheat from the United States. The ending of the slave trade and the end of the Napoleonic Wars, both around the turn of the century, had upset this cycle. The soaring cost of lumber in Europe had offered a new profitable opportunity to bring it from the forests of Canada, but something to carry on the westward leg of the voyage would greatly improve profits, and the dramatic increase in emigrants to the United States, led by the Irish, in the mid 1880s, fit the bill very nicely. In just a few years, the new kind of human cargo was generating more profits than the valuable Canadian lumber on the eastward leg of the journey.

This new profit opportunity generated a rush to build new ships and/or convert old ships to meet the growing demand. Brand new American packet ships of over 1,000 tons with triple decks were built in the late 1840s specifically for the emigrant trade. They could carry about 400 passengers in relative comfort. But the fleet of ships also included the *Elizabeth and Sarah* which had been at sea for 83 years when it achieved infamy in late 1846 as an outbreak of typhoid fever claimed over 20 lives (including the captain) among the almost 300 passengers (almost twice the recommended level) on board. The passengers were jammed together for several weeks in unsanitary conditions with little food or clean water.

The profits were so attractive (even though fares were as low as $10 in United States currency) that tiny ships like the *Hannah*, basically a ship used only near the coast, was converted for ocean travel. The *Hannah* was only 59 feet long (about four car lengths), and had a crew of only six. She made five trips to New York in the period from various Irish ports, carrying

50–60 passengers jammed into her single hold for periods as long as two months. The urge to emigrate to the United States was so intense that one of the ships arriving early in the process, the *Perseverance*, reported that soon after her arrival in New York, in May of 1846, the entire ship's crew had deserted into New York City.

However, New York City was not the only destination. Many emigrants from Ireland traveled to Canada. This was because the fares were cheaper as the trip was somewhat or fully subsidized by the British government which was trying both to remove starving Irish from their doorstep and to populate Canada. Many Irish took a vow to settle in Canada, but once safely across the ocean, they headed south to the United States. The weather was not as cold, jobs were more readily available, and the immigrants were no longer under the rule of the hated British king. The result was that Boston had only a tenth of the direct traffic as that arriving in New York, but Boston was still swollen with Irish immigrants coming from Canada.

1854 — California Supreme Court Ruling — The high degree of racial discrimination that would develop against the relatively small group of Chinese immigrants in California was highlighted by a ruling from the California Supreme Court (People v. Hall) that a white man charged with murder cannot be convicted on the testimony of a Chinese person. Two years earlier the entry of perhaps as many as 20,000 Chinese immigrants into mining regions brought back a Foreign Miner's Tax Law aimed at the Chinese. Such discrimination would continue even after a primarily Chinese labor force would build the Central Pacific Railroad part of the transcontinental railroad in the 1860s (see entry for May 10, 1869). The Chinese were found by the railroad to be clearly superior workers compared to native Californians.

1854 — Railroad Immigration Promotions — The Illinois Central railroad was the first railroad to aggressively recruit immigrants to come to its region and buy land it had under development. The railroad sent special agents to the German states and the Scandinavian countries. These men attended such things as fairs and church services, and they arranged meetings, advertised in local newspapers, and promised great results to prospective settlers. They helped secure ocean passage, and also arranged free railroad transportation to Illinois for prospective land buyers.

For those who bought, the Illinois Central provided long-term financing at an interest rate of six percent, gave discounts to those who farmed the land for future crop shipments on the railroad, and agreed to pay all taxes on the land until the land-buying payments were complete. Such inducements caused many immigrants to buy railroad land rather than homesteading free government acreage, especially where it appeared the railroad offered choicer properties.

The Illinois Central had essentially completed its efforts by 1870 when other railroads began belatedly to follow its example. Ultimately, the efforts of the Burlington line resulted in the sale of three million acres of land in Iowa and Nebraska, and the Northern Pacific railroad was credited with doubling the population of Minnesota, the Dakotas, Montana, and the Pacific Northwest between 1880 and 1900.

1855 — Castle Garden— Realizing that the large number of immigrants coming into its harbor needed some sort of defined place to land and catch their breath, so to speak, New York established an immigrant depot at a place called Castle Garden. It was near the Battery where it protruded into New York harbor. At this location immigrants could be free of exploitation (often by members of their country of origin who had preceded them), change their foreign money, arrange for accommodations, buy railroad tickets if they were headed further inland, and learn where they could best seek employment.

Castle Garden gave way to Ellis Island which was opened in 1892 (see entry for January 1, 1892) when the Federal Government finally decided to take over the responsibility for processing immigrants arriving in New York (and elsewhere). Ellis Island was much larger and had more resources than Castle Garden, but the latter was an initial step in an attempt to bring more order to the immigration process as immigration in total grew steadily to a rate of 200,000 persons per month. It was the threat of closing down Castle Garden that finally brought Congress to offer some assistance in processing immigrants to the states in August 1882 (see entry). All previous attempts by the states to collect funds to help process immigrants had been ruled unconstitutional on the same grounds as the "Passenger Case" of 1849 (see entry for 1849) which held that only Congress could regulate immigration. The frustration of the states with the concept that only Congress can regulate immigration and the fact that Congress can rarely seem to get its act together to do so has a long history of over 150 years.

1855 — Know Nothings — The anti-immigrant group known as the "Know Nothings" reached its peak membership of about one million white adult protestant males (this represented over 10 percent of the potential electorate considering that only about six million men had voted in the Presidential election of 1852). The movement was eventually known as the "Know Nothings" because as a "secret society" its members were instructed to reply "I know nothing" if queried about the group's activities. Their rise to a million members took place in a little over two years. The Know Nothings were primarily an anti–Catholic group, and thus they were very much opposed to the rise in Irish immigrants, nearly all of whom were Catholic, and the parallel rise in German immigrants, many of whom were noted as Catholics.

In the elections of 1854 and 1855, Know-Nothing candidates were elected as eight governors, over 100 Congressmen, mayors of Boston, Philadelphia, and Chicago, and thousands of other locally elected positions. Under the banner of the American Party, the Know-Nothings backed ex-president Millard Fillmore for the presidency in 1856. Fillmore got 800,000 votes, about 20 percent of the electorate, but won only the state of Maryland in the Electoral College and James Buchanan won the presidency.

The Know-Nothings faded after their 1856 defeat, and after Abraham Lincoln, who loathed the group, was elected president in 1860, the movement basically died away. However, anti–Catholic rhetoric, especially as directed at immigrants, would exist in politics for many decades more.

April 12, 1861 — The outbreak of the Civil War in the United States drove immigration below 100,000 annually in 1861 and 1862. It was the first time since 1844 that total immigration fell below 100,000, and it would be the last time until the depression year of 1931.

May 20, 1862 — The Homestead Act was passed, and it was followed seven weeks later by the Land Grant Act on July 7. The essence of the

Homestead Act was the granting of free farmland in the west to settlers who would live on and improve the land for five years, while the Land Grant Act was the first of many that gave public land to the states and also granted Federal Aid to build educational facilities that grew into the state university systems. The absence of southern legislators due to the Civil War helped the new laws pass in Congress.

The significance of the Acts to immigrants was that they were yet another vehicle through which many immigrants, who could never hope to own land in their countries of origin, could do so in the United States. Further, the "Land Act" schools were aimed at less well-off citizens who could break the concept that higher education was only for the elite, and many immigrants would later realize a family dream of one of their own obtaining a college degree. All of these items were factors in yet more immigrants coming to the United States throughout the rest of the century and into the next.

1862—The "Anti-Coolie" Act discouraged the coming of Chinese immigrants to California, and instituted special taxes on employers who hired Chinese workers. Chinese immigrants to California were hardly a tenth of the number of immigrants arriving on the East Coast at the time, but they faced violent discrimination in California, and Congress was anxious to be as supportive of California as possible to prevent California from even thinking about joining the states that had seceded from the union. This kind of thinking also helped get the transcontinental railroad underway, which ironically, Chinese workers played by far the largest part in building in California and from the West Coast towards the east. Another much-maligned immigrant group, Irish-Americans, played the biggest part in building the line from Omaha towards the west (see entry for May 10, 1869).

July 1863— Riots against the Civil War draft broke out in New York City during the period from July 13 through 16. Many immigrants who opposed compulsory military service were involved, and about 1,000 people were killed or wounded. But mobs blaming blacks hanged some blacks as the riots progressed.

1867 — Tenements— The New York Tenement law of 1867 was enacted. It was one of the first housing codes in the United States. It applied only to New York City, but as New York City had by far the largest tenement facilities in the nation, it became a model for nearly all other cities with large tenement installations. This meant in essence for all cities with large immigrant populations, because it was the steady inflow of immigrants seeking some place to live that drove the building of large tenement installations to meet the demand.

The 1867 law became known as the "Old Law" to differentiate it from new laws enacted in 1879, 1888, 1889, and especially in 1901. Each new law was somewhat more stringent (for landlords) than the one before, but a law with "real teeth" and substantial improvements (such as indoor plumbing) was not established until 1901 (see entry for April 12, 1901). Tenement life was a notable part of the early days in the United States for many immigrants, and the details of such a life ultimately became a national scandal.

The influx of Irish and German immigrants (see entry for 1847), many of whom stayed in the New York City area, drove the need for the building and/or conversion of existing buildings to tenements. The population of New York City increased by 65 percent in the 1840s (from 312,710 to 515,547) and by another 58 percent in the 1850s (from 515,547 to 813,669). Both groups tended to settle on the Lower East Side of Manhattan; the Germans in an area called "Kliendeutschland" or "Little Germany." The Germans tended to have more assets than other immigrants and thus lived in the "nicer" area of what was actually a teeming slum from top to bottom where future immigrants would also settle.

The Lower East Side of Manhattan became famous — or infamous — for its incredibly crowded tenements. The city area was originally laid out from farmland in the late 18th century, using lots that were 25 feet wide and 100 feet deep. These lots were quite suitable for the single family row homes originally built there in the early 1800s. But as New York City dramatically increased in population in the 1840s and 1850s due to the arrival of masses of immigrants as noted in the paragraph above, the home owners on the Lower East Side moved to the more fashionable Northern part of Manhattan. Builders then began to convert the single-family homes into dwellings for multiple families. The result was buildings five-to-six stories high on the relatively small 25 × 100 foot lots, and the intended occupancy was 20 families or more where a single family used to live.

As early as 1843, the "Association for Improving the Conditions of the Poor" described these early Tenements as defective in size and arrangement, water supply, warmth and ventilation, with yards, sinks, and sewage in generally bad condition. Similar surveys in 1864 by an activist group called the "Council of Hygiene and Public Health" found that 495,492 people lived in tenements in New York City. This was more than half the population of the entire city. In the Lower East Side, the population density was 240,000 people per square mile, which the council proclaimed was the highest density in the history of the earth to that point in time.

A typical tenement had five stories and housed 20 families in three-room apartments laid out four apartments to a floor, two in the front of the building and two in back. Reached by an unlighted wooden staircase running through the building (it was at least a source of ventilation), the average apartment contained about 325 square feet for the typically seven or more people occupying the three rooms (only one of which was officially designated as a bedroom). Only the front room of each apartment received light and ventilation, although some bedrooms had casement windows opening into the hallway. There was no toilet, shower, or bath, or for that matter necessarily any water supply running directly into the apartment. The "privies" for each building were located in the back yard, and may or may not been connected to a local sewer.

The 1867 law required at least one privy per 20 people with connection to a local sewer as available. It also required one three-foot square transom over each interior bedroom door for light and ventilation. A subsequent law in 1879, as amended in 1888 and 1879, required all rooms to have access to air, and required flush toilets in the backyard with individual compartments to which each tenant had a key for his personal compartment. As noted, more substantial changes (including indoor plumbing) came with the law of 1901, which was strongly contested by landlords (see entry for April 12, 1901).

1867 — Qing Government— The Qing Government of China hired Anson Burlingame essentially as an agent to develop better trade relations with the United States and to be advocate for better treatment of Chinese nationals in the United States. Burlingame did manage to initiate negotiations at the ambassador level that recognized the rights of citizens of both nations to migrate from one country to another, and he hoped that the 14th Amendment, ratified in 1868 (see next entry) and written to cover freed slaves from the Civil War would aid the Chinese in their efforts to gain a path to citizenship.

The 14th Amendment stated that "all persons born or naturalized in the United States, and subject to the jurisdiction thereof, are citizens of the United States and of the state wherein they reside." However, the subsequent Naturalization Act of 1870 (see entry for July 1870) still limited citizenship to whites and "persons of African descent."

July 28, 1868— The 14th Amendment was promulgated by the secretary of state of the United States as having been approved by Congress and ratified by a sufficient number of states to become part of the Constitution and to have the effect of law. Congress wrote the 14th Amendment essentially for the protection of the newly freed slaves who were rapidly encountering discrimination of all types by the southern states of the old confederacy. The significant parts of the Amendment declared anyone born in the United States to automatically be a citizen of the United States, and "any person" in the United States eligible for equal protection of the law. For the freed slaves the 14th Amendment would not necessarily provide in its time all of its intended protections, but it would ultimately, as interpreted by future Supreme Courts, would become the basis for the desegregation of public schools in the United States in 1954, and the basis for the elimination of gender bias in nearly every aspect of life in the United States (including such things as the admission of women to military academies and to active duty in the armed forces). Into this realm of unintended consequences would come an important role in the late 1900s when the amendment was applied to cases involving illegal immigrants. The fact that anyone born in the United States is automatically a citizen would encourage pregnant women residing in Mexico to slip quickly across the border to hospitals in the San Diego area, for example, give birth (free of charge), and then return to Mexico with a child who was a citizen of the United States and eligible for certain benefits anytime they returned to the United States. Illegal immigrants who came to the United States fulltime also used the amendment and had children born here who were automatically citizens. The child was then eligible for certain welfare benefits, which the illegal immigrants would collect as the child's custodians. Applicable laws would make the birth of the child free as well as other medical services the illegal immigrants would obtain from emergency rooms forbidden to deny services just because of an inability to pay.

To complete the basic list of benefits "demanded" by illegal immigrants, the 14th Amendment was interpreted by the Supreme Court in 1982 (see entry for June 15, 1982) to require states to offer free elementary and secondary education to children of illegal immigrants under the "equal protection of the laws" clause. The court emphasized that although the illegal immigrants were not citizens, they were "people" and thus eligible for the free education provided to other citizens.

Thus, as an unintended consequence, the 14th Amendment became a magnet for illegal immigrants a little more than a century after it was written. The often repeated claim that the illegal immigrants came here to work to survive and not for the corollary benefits sounded very hollow in cases where the children of illegal immigrants were denied cheaper tuition as an in state resident to go on to college. The illegal immigrant parents complained of "unfair" treatment and made it clear that higher education benefits were a prime goal when they originally came here illegally.

But the writers of the 14th Amendment could not foresee the uses it would be put to over 100 years in the future. The law of unintended consequences is a law with a very long reach into areas no one can originally imagine.

May 10, 1869— The famous "Golden Spike" was driven at Promontory Point in Utah to complete the transcontinental railroad as the Union Pacific line being built from the east-to west met the Central Pacific line being built from west-to-east. The decision to build the transcontinental had been made by Congress in 1862, once again taking advantage of the absence of southern legislators due to the Civil War. The bill authorizing construction of the line was deliberately written to encourage a race between the Union Pacific and the Central Pacific (of California) to be sure the line was finished in good time by 1876, with the best builder getting the best payment.

The line was finished in half the time allotted, and the Central Pacific essentially won the race, even after having to build and tunnel through

1869

the formidable Sierra Nevada mountains in California. The significance of the line from an immigration point of view was that the Central Pacific part was built by the much-maligned (on the West Coast) Chinese immigrants, and the Union Pacific workforce was predominately made up of almost as greatly-maligned (on the East Coast) Irish-Americans. There were great financial scandals after the line was completed, with many members of Congress caught with their hands in the cookie jar, but that didn't change the fact that the great success of building the line (and economically it was a very great success) was due to two sets of much-maligned immigrants.

The Irish immigrants had arrived in great numbers prior to the construction of the line (see entry for 1847), and although they were instrumental in building roads, canals, and early railroads, they were greeted in Boston with help-wanted signs reading NINA (No Irish Need Apply) and real estate transactions containing clauses forbidding the sale of the property in perpetuity to any person or descendent of the Irish race.

On the West Coast, Chinese immigrants were treated even worse as part of the "Yellow Peril" feared by all Nativists. But they were hired in desperation by the Central Pacific railroad for the tedious and dangerous task of building a railroad through and over the imposing Sierra Nevadas. California citizens would accept the job, and then desert the rail line as soon as they got delivered into the high Sierras from where they could go prospecting for gold or silver in California or Nevada with the cash stake they had collected from the railroad. Citizens interested in mining were not interested in the exhausting railroad task. The Chinese immigrants, although generally small in stature, worked excellently in groups and performed the task with efficiency never seen before.

Both the Union Pacific and the Central Pacific eventually accumulated workforces approaching 13,000 men at their peaks. The Irish-Americans had the biggest single representation of the many ethnic groups working for the Union Pacific, and the Chinese comprised 80 percent of the Central Pacific workforce. There were few "laborers" who were not Chinese. The Irish-Americans eventually were absorbed into the nation's citizenry. The Chinese were "rewarded" 13 years later in 1882 with a racist law banning all Chinese immigrants (see entry for May 6, 1882). Critics of the new law noted that the Chinese immigrants were not asked to tear up their substantial contribution to the transcontinental railroad before they were banned from entering the United States in the future.

July 1870— The Naturalization Act of 1870 expanded citizenship rights to both whites and blacks, but Asians were still barred on the basis of color. However, the Fifteenth Amendment, ratified this year, granted voting rights to citizens without regard to "race, color, or previous condition of servitude." Discrimination against Asians remained high even though blacks, at least legally, were on a par with all other citizens.

Among the tide of immigrants arriving in the United States in this year was Jacob Riis from Denmark. Riis later pioneered photojournalism, and in 1890 he would write the book *How the Other Half Lives* about life in the tenement slums in New York City. This book would help call attention to the continued abuses of tenement life and support the tenement laws of 1901 (see entry for April 12, 1901) that attempted to improve living conditions for tenement inhabitants (mostly immigrants).

1871— The Senate ratified the Burlingame Treaty (see entry for 1867, Qing Government) with China. Although this treaty recognized "the inherent and inalienable right of man to change his home and allegiance" and "a mutual advantage of ... free migration," the treaty added "nothing contained herein should be held to confer naturalization ... upon the subjects of China in the United States." The apparent split in the treaty unfortunately was followed through by the United States Congress, which a decade later passed the Chinese Exclusion Act (see entry for May 6, 1882) which completely barred all Chinese citizens from the United States.

Part of the apparent contradiction was due to the fact that the so-called "Chinese question" was primarily a West Coast concern, and the Congress simply was going along with what they saw as West Coast concerns to be sure West Coast voters would not hinder their re-election campaigns.

The Burlingame Treaty was renegotiated during the 1870s and by October of 1881, it contained language about suspending the coming or residence of Chinese laborers. It added a ten-year period of possible suspension of admission of the Chinese, and this finally became the Chinese Exclusion Act signed on May 6, 1882 (see entry).

1873

1873 — A new era in providing transportation for immigrants was marked by the fact that as of the year 1873, over 96 percent of all immigrants arriving in New York traveled by steamship. As recently as 1856, over 96 percent of all immigrants arriving in New York came in sailing vessels. This conversion to steamship reduced the time of travel from one-to-three months to a much more easily tolerated ten days. The accommodations were similarly much more comfortable as the steamships were generally built from scratch for passenger use rather than being converted from freight use.

The incidence of outbreaks of typhoid and cholera on board were also reduced, but this was primarily a result of the reduced sailing time rather than a dramatic increase in sanitation from the old sailing ships. The sailing ships per se did not deserve the accusations of "fever ships" that grew up around them as greatly increased immigrant trade began in the earlier 1800s (see entry for 1840). There were certainly many incidents of poor sanitation causing cholera and typhoid among travelers suffering from malnutrition. But we are talking about thousands of ships sailing yearly, carrying a large percentage of poor and unhealthy people. Many immigrants were already carrying infections when they boarded the ships, and in several weeks at sea in very crowded conditions, the diseases were easily spread. Only 10 days at sea in less crowded conditions greatly reduced this effect.

The universal use of the steamship soon produced fierce competition between Britain and Germany in providing steamship services across the Atlantic, and the potential immigrants benefited as usual from the competition in terms of lower fares and the ease of arrangements from door-to-port that went along with them. This ultimately expanded the source of immigrants to central, eastern, and southern Europe (Austria-Hungary, Russia, and Italy) that became the prime source of immigrants to the United States soon after 1890.

Further, the relatively simple crossings provided by the steamships led to the development of a flow of temporary immigrants with certain skills who came to the United States to take advantage of large wage differences between the United States and their areas during certain seasons, and then in essence returned home for the winter. The wage differences were large enough to cover the costs of what was now an almost casual ocean crossing and temporary living expenses while leaving a tidy profit. This "temporary" immigrant flow became substantial enough that by the depression of the 1930s there were years when more people left the United States than arrived.

The ease of steamship travel also encouraged individual states and various railroad companies to advertise directly in Europe for immigrants to fill what were then the large empty spaces in areas west of the Mississippi River. But these entities also regularly advertised in the United States for the same purpose, so it is difficult to tell if their success in filling these areas with new immigrants (and they were very successful in doing so) was a result of directly attracting new immigrants to the United States or redirecting them west once they arrived. The lure of available land was the key factor in either case.

Whatever the situation, there is no doubt that the advent of universal steamship travel played a major role in creating the record numbers of immigrants that arrived in the United States between 1880 and 1914. The number of immigrants grew so large that the United States government decided it was "too much of a good thing."

March 1875— The Page Act was passed by the Congress of the United States to address the issue of immigration from China and Japan. The law required migrants from "Oriental" countries to be processed at the port of departure by representatives of consulates of the United States. The intention was to deny departure rights to those who were "obnoxious."

The real intention of the act was to screen out prostitutes and forced "Coolie" laborers. But it substantially reduced opportunities for all Asian women to enter the United States, and ultimately created hardships for the wives of immigrants already in the United States.

1881— This year marked the beginning of the peak of German immigration. During the years from 1881 through 1885, one million German immigrants arrived in the United States. The Germans had overtaken the Irish as the most numerous immigrants to arrive to date in the United States, and would remain so until overtaken on an annual basis by the Italians early in the new century.

On an overall basis, between about 1840 and 1920, the leading immi-

1882

grant groups were about 6 million Germans, 4.75 million Italians, and 4.5 million Irish. On an ethnic basis between 1881 and 1920, two million Jews from Eastern Europe immigrated to the United States.

May 6, 1882 — Congress passed the Chinese Exclusion Act, which completely barred immigration from China. The act flowed directly from 1880 revisions to the Burlingame Treaty (see entry for 1871). These 1880 revisions permitted the United States to suspend immigration of the Chinese, and Congress acted quickly (for them) to enact the Exclusion Law in 1882.

The act excluded all Chinese laborers from immigrating to the United States for a period of ten years. Amendments made in 1884 tightened provisions that had allowed previous Chinese immigrants to leave and return again, and clarified the fact that the law applied to all ethnic Chinese regardless of their country of origin. The act would be renewed in 1892 at the end of the first 10-year period (see entry for the Geary Act of May 1892), and at the end of the second 10-year period in 1902, it would be renewed again for an indefinite period. The Act would finally be repealed in 1943 by the Magnuson Act (see entry for December 17, 1943) with a symbolic quota of 105 Chinese allowed per year with China now being an ally of the United States in World War II.

Congressional debate had been going on for decade prior to 1882 about the "Chinese question." The issue of exclusion was pushed primarily by Californians who had discriminated strongly against the Chinese since they began to show up in California in the 1850s to pursue gold strikes. Many were "sojourners" who wanted to accumulate about $400 to return to China and live like emperors in the desperately poor country.

The number of Chinese grew slowly in California until they eventually became the backbone of the Central Pacific railroad building the western end of the transcontinental railroad (see entry for May 10, 1869). When the Central Pacific job was complete and more than 10,000 Chinese laborers returned to the West Coast circa 1870, efforts intensified in California to regulate the immigration of all Chinese. The result was the Chinese Exclusion Act, which was the first immigration bill to target a specific ethic group, and was as racist a bill as ever passed by an American Congress. But unfortunately it was not the last on both counts.

During the time the Exclusion Law was in effect, more than 55,000 Chinese immigrants were processed through Angel Island (see entry for January 1910) in San Francisco Bay. Most tried to take advantage of the few exceptions to the Exclusion Law. These exceptions included children of Chinese who were born in the United States and thus automatically were citizens of the United States. The San Francisco earthquake and fire of 1906 destroyed many birth certificate records, opening the door for those who used counterfeit documents and memorized histories of Chinese citizens to portray themselves as children of Chinese citizens. They were known as "paper sons" (and rarely "paper daughters") when they successfully used this approach to enter the United States in spite of its Chinese Exclusion Law.

August 1882 — Bowing to pressure from the states to assist in the cost of processing immigrants (the states in the northeast were most vocal), Congress passed a law called the Act to Regulate Immigration. The act authorized a head tax of fifty cents on each alien to help pay for processing. Further, the law provided for the exclusion of "convicts, lunatics, idiots, and those liable to become a public charge." The clinching pressure came when New York City threatened to close down the Castle Garden facility it had opened in 1855 (see entry for 1855–Castle Garden).

December 31, 1882 — There were 788,902 immigrants recorded as entering the United States in the year 1882. This was the largest number of immigrants received in one year in the country's history through 1882. The number would not be exceeded until 1903, when the United States was building up to its all-time peak of new arrivals in 1907 (see entry for December 31, 1907).

1882 was the peak year for "old" immigrant arrivals, with 87 percent of the record number of immigrants coming from the countries of northern and western Europe and 13 percent coming from southern and eastern Europe. By the all-time record year of 1907, the percentages would be 19.3 percent "old" immigrants and 80.7 "new" immigrants from southern and eastern Europe. The year 1896 would mark the first time the "new" immigrants would outnumber the "old" immigrants. Racial, ethnic, and religious bias against the "new" immigrants would lead to restrictive laws against immigration in the first decade of the twentieth century. By 1931,

1885

immigration would fall below 100,000 annually for the first time since 1844 and stay would there until 1946.

Also, by 1930, the "old" and "new" immigrants were relatively well balanced in the nation's history. About 15 million immigrants had arrived in the United States since its beginning and 1890, and another 20 million had arrived between 1890 and 1930. The first group of 15 million was predominately "old" immigrants from northern and western Europe, while the second group of 20 million was predominately "new" immigrants from southern and eastern Europe.

February 1885— Congress passed the so-called Foran Act barring the immigration of "contract labor." The Foran Act was passed under pressure from labor unions that saw such labor as being used as "strikebreakers" in labor disputes. The Act was full of exceptions, and actually applied to relatively few immigrants. However, the Act was indicative of a growing resistance to immigration in general, and a national change in outlook (led by Nativists) that immigration was not so much a response to a need but rather a growing problem that needed a solution. The Foran Act reversed an 1864 law authorizing contract labor, and was a sign of more restrictive laws to come. There were additional laws passed regarding this issue in 1887, 1888, and 1891.

May 1886— What became known as the "Haymarket Riot" took place in Chicago. Strikes and rallies focusing on the demand for an eight-hour day for workers ended with the police breaking up a mass union meeting in Haymarket Square. A bomb was thrown into a group of policemen, killing one instantly and six others later. Shots were fired between workers and the police, and the death tool grew to a total of ten, with scores injured.

The Haymarket affair ended a decade of violence between unionists and law enforcement dating from the "Molly Maguires" killings and subsequent hangings that started in 1875 in the coalfields of Pennsylvania. Various anarchists were accused (and later executed) for the Haymarket Riots, and public opinion was easily turned against foreign-born "radicals" who had come to the United States as immigrants. It was claimed that such radicals were always involved in the violent battles between the unions and law enforcement, and it was the foreign born who took the lead in organizing radical elements within the unions. Demands were made for more careful screening of immigrants, and a restrictive tide was beginning just as immigrants reached a then-historical peak in the 1881–90 decade.

October 28, 1886— The Statue of Liberty, which has stood as a symbol of freedom and immigration for over 120 years, was dedicated on this date in New York City harbor. Originally known as "Liberty Enlightening the World," the statue was designed by French sculptor Frederic Bartholdi and given to the United States by France to commemorate the friendship between the two nations.

As early as Washington's Birthday on February 22, 1877, Congress approved the use of a site called Bedloe's Island (suggested by Bartholdi) in New York harbor. It took until 1884 for the statue to be completed, and it was presented to the American minister to France on July 4, 1884, to commemorate the Anniversary of the American Revolution. The cornerstone for the pedestal that would support the statue was laid on August 5, 1884. It took additional funds to complete the pedestal than were initially allotted, and Joseph Pulitzer, owner of the famous newspaper *New York World,* raised these in a series of appeals to readers.

The statue arrived in June of 1885 dismantled into 214 separate packages. It was reassembled over the next 16 months, and the last rivet was driven on October 28, 1886 when President Grover Cleveland dedicated the statue and its pedestal. About 15 million immigrants would subsequently view the Statue of Liberty as their initial greeting to the United States in the next 40 years.

The Statue of Liberty and nearby Ellis Island, opened in 1892 (see entry for January 1, 1892) were the symbol of immigration in what many call the "Golden Age" of immigration, but as is often the case, the reality is somewhat different than the myth. Immigration came to a peak as these two symbols arrived on the scene (in millions there were 5.2 in 1880–89, 3.7 in 1890–1899, 8.2 in 1900–09, 6.3 in 1910–19, and 4.3 in 1920–29), but just as the Statue of Liberty was being dedicated there were rumbles of displeasure with immigration in the nation. The numbers were growing far beyond previous years, and the immigrants were primarily from southern Europe (Italy) and eastern Europe (Russia and Slovakia) rather than western Europe.

1886

Restrictive legislation would arise in Congress between the late 1880s and 1920s, and the Golden Age of immigration would come to an end in the 1920s. The use of foreign embassies to issue visas would reduce the number of immigrants coming through the Ellis Island/Statue of Liberty gateway, and both would become museums and national monuments as time went by. However, the symbolism of the Statue of Liberty showing the way to a new life for millions of desperately poor immigrants would survive indefinitely.

The words of the poem by Emma Lazarus, engraved on the pedestal supporting the statue, and later immortalized in song by Irving Berlin, summarized the best hopes of the United States as a haven for poor immigrants, regardless of later issues in history. The last words of the poem, that were later set to music, read:

> Give me your tired, your poor,
> Your huddled masses yearning to breathe free.
> The wretched refuse of your teeming shore.
> Send these, the homeless, tempest-tost to me,
> I lift my lamp beside the golden door!

1886— Another notable event in the year of 1886 was the immigration to the United States from Lithuania of feminist Emma Goldman, who for the next 30 years was an infamous anarchist. She was finally deported to Russia in 1917 during World War I for conspiring to obstruct the draft. Noisy anarchists like Goldman were a significant factor in the restrictive immigration laws passed in the United States in the first 25 years of the 1900s.

1888— Congress passed the so-called "Scott" Act. Named for Representative William L. Scott of Pennsylvania, this act unilaterally cancelled certificates of return for those Chinese who had been required to leave the United States by the 1882 Exclusion Act (see entry for May 6, 1882), but were granted certificates for the conditions of the return. President Cleveland signed the Scott Act into law about a month before the 1888 election. William Scott happened to be the campaign manager for Cleveland in the upcoming election. Cleveland noted that although the provision of the certificates had been agreed upon previously, he was justified in eliminating them due to the difficulty of assimilating Chinese into the United States. The Chinese challenged the position in court, but the court upheld that the government could change established treaties and in the case where the laws of the treaty and the new law were in conflict, the law of the land that would prevail would be whichever came later.

In spite of Cleveland's last-minute maneuver, he lost the Presidential election of 1888 to Benjamin Harrison. However, Cleveland beat Harrison in a rematch in 1892, becoming the answer to a trivia question as to who was the only sitting president in United States history to lose a presidential election and then come back later to win again.

March 23, 1889 — President Benjamin Harrison issued a Proclamation that opened two million acres of "unassigned lands" in Oklahoma for settlement under the provisions of the Homestead Act of 1862 (see entry for May 20, 1862). These lands were considered by many to be the best "public" lands now available in the United States (they were previously in "Indian Territory"). The result was that many groups across the entire United States started planning to make claims on the new lands, including many immigrants. The Homestead Act permitted settlers to receive title after a five-year period of living on, and improving, the land. Impoverished farmers, common laborers, professional men, and politicians all competed with immigrants to find a way to eventually claim ownership of the prime land.

By late spring of 1889, a large number of would-be settlers were camped in Kansas' border towns. Other "Boomers," as they were called, came from the south and west to camp along the other borders of the Oklahoma Territory. Sites along the Santa Fe Railroad that had been built through the Oklahoma Territory in 1886–7 were considered choice spots as later town sites, and many settlers planned to enter the race by way of the railroad. This was an unfortunate decision, because it cost them dearly in some cases as the Supreme Court later decided this was an illegal entry. Others entered the Territory early and hid out until the official time. They were known as "sooners" a nickname later applied to sports teams at the University of Oklahoma.

United States troops were supposed to monitor the run, but they were generally too few in number and too spread out to do the task

1889

effectively. At noon on April 22, 1889, an estimated 50,000 people began the rush across the borders of the Oklahoma Territory. Some hardy single women were included, but blacks had to hold back and then come in after the initial rush. All were later known as "eighty-niners." Claimants determined the location of their choice based on surveyors' cornerstone markers, planted a stake indicating their claim, and then rushed to the land office to register their claim. The day was incredibly chaotic, but within about nine hours, an estimated 11,000 agricultural homesteads were claimed among the 2 million acres available. The area became officially known as the Oklahoma Territory in 1890, and as adjoining Indian tribal lands were opened to settlement the territory became the 46th state of the Union — Oklahoma — in 1907. Ironically, only a little over 25 years later many "Okies" would lose their lands to the "Dust Bowl" of the Great Depression and begin a forced exodus to California.

1889— Jane Adams and Ellen Gates Starr founded what was known as Hull House in Chicago. Both women were social activists, and Hull House provided many services for the poor, including many immigrants.

1890— Census— The Census of 1890 was the first census to observe a generally continuous string of white settlements across the United States from both east to west and north to south. Thus, it was called by many as the census that showed that the frontier had disappeared in the United States. The nation was now a "settled" country, although its overall population density was still quite low, and there was plenty of space between existing settlements for new ones.

Approximately 15 million immigrants had arrived in the United States between the Revolution of 1776 and 1890. However, even though the country was considered "settled" by 1890, another 60 million immigrants would arrive between 1890 and today.

The same Census could be used to confirm recent trends showing immigration from northern and western Europe was beginning to decline while that from southern and eastern Europe was substantially increasing (see entries for December 31, 1882 and December 31, 1907).

1890— Manufacturing Issues— Many manufacturing changes in the United States evolved throughout the end of the nineteenth century, and the new immigrants they utilized are often defined by the phrase "before and after 1890." For example, in the bituminous coal fields, workers experienced in pick or hand mining were no longer needed after mechanical cutters began to be used on the coal faces. In cotton manufacturing, a period of brief training was enough for a new immigrant to operate automatic looms and ring-spinning frames.

The result was that whereas as the coal mines of Pennsylvania before 1890 had been primarily been occupied by American-born workers or those of the English Isles or Germany, after 1890 the primary workers became Slovak, Hungarian, Polish and Italian. Similarly, in the textile manufacturing areas of New England, the workforce that before 1890 was primarily British, Irish, and French-Canadian became Polish, Portuguese, Greek and Syrian. In the garment trades of big cities, German, Bohemian, and Irish stock were replaced by Russian Jewish workers and Italians.

There is the question of cause-and-effect as the mix of new immigrants after 1890 switched to southern and eastern Europeans of limited skills just when manufacturing in the United States was relying much more on new machines than personal skills, but the merging of the two issues was probably inevitable once the steamships made immigration much easier for the new immigrants (see entry for 1873). The development of new manufacturing equipment not only made it possible to use unskilled workers to a much greater extent, it made it necessary to use (lower paid) unskilled workers to recoup the cost of the investment in the new equipment designs.

The dramatic industrial expansion in the United States in the late nineteenth century not only was primarily sustainable thanks to the influx of the "new" immigrants from southern and eastern Europe. The growth of industry not only easily absorbed the large number of new immigrants, it provided the immigrants existing prior to the new influx with the opportunity to climb the supervisory/management ladder to better paying jobs. By 1910 the Dillingham Commission (see entries for December 31, 1907 and 1911–Dillingham) found that in 21 industries it studied, 58 percent of all employees were foreign born, with two-thirds of those from southern and eastern Europe. In industries such as clothing manufacturing, textiles, coal mining, and slaughtering and meat packing, the proportions were even higher.

The huge influx of the "new" immigrants was actually a win-win sit-

1891

uation for the building of the industrial might of the United States before World War I, but racial and ethnic discrimination would cause the new immigrants to become the reason for the restrictive immigration laws developed in the first 25 years of the 20th century.

1891—Congress created the Immigration and Naturalization Service (INS) within the Treasury Department to administer federal laws regarding the admission, exclusion, and deportation of all aliens, as well as the naturalization of aliens presently residing lawfully within the United States. One of the early acts of the INS was to open the immigrant screening station on Ellis Island in 1892 (see entry for January 1, 1892).

Congress also modified the immigration law to exclude "persons suffering from a loathsome or a dangerous contagious disease," those convicted of a "misdemeanor involving moral turpitude," and polygamists.

January 1, 1892—The Federal government officially opened its immigration station on Ellis Island in New York Harbor, just off the coast of New Jersey. Prior to this date, the individual states bore the responsibility for processing immigrants, as previously mentioned. But as New York was the prime destination of many immigrants of this era, the city was overwhelmed and the Federal government finally stepped in to help, after New York had threatened to close its Castle Garden facility (see entry for 1855).

Over the years, Ellis Island was enlarged from its original 3.3 acres to 27.3 acres by using landfill from the ballast of ships, the excavations for the New York subway system, and similar places. About 8 million immigrants had been processed through New York harbor prior to the existence of the Ellis Island facility; and another 12 million were processed through Ellis Island from 1892 to 1954 (mostly by 1920, when the immigration processing task was taken over primarily by the numerous airport facilities throughout the United States). The year 1907 was the peak year for Ellis Island, with just over 1 million immigrants processed. The single biggest day occurred on April 17, 1907, with 11,747 processed.

The first person processed through the Ellis Island facility in 1892 was an Irish girl named Annie Moore, who happened to be celebrating her 15th birthday at the same time as she entered Ellis Island. She was given a ten-dollar gold Liberty coin (an impressive amount of money for a new immigrant at the time) in recognition of her being the first person to be registered there. This was probably the most valuable birthday present she received that day. Ellis Island is now a museum that is part of the Statue of Liberty National Monument (see entry for October 28, 1886). The museum attracts two million visitors annually.

May 1892— As the original term of exclusion was about to expire, Congress passed the Geary Act, which extended the exclusion of the Chinese for another ten years and placed even harsher restrictions upon Chinese person living in the United States. They were required to carry at all times a resident permit, a sort of international passport. In a reversal of the concept that a man is innocent until proven guilty, the Congress stated that "any Chinese person or person of Chinese descent" was deemed to be in the country illegally unless he or she could demonstrate otherwise.

Further, Chinese were barred from serving as witnesses in court, and from receiving bail in habeas corpus proceedings. The Geary Act tried to make any Chinese person as near a non-person as possible. The law was challenged in court, but ultimately upheld by the Supreme Court. Anti-Chinese bias was now firmly established in the entire United States.

1894— The Immigration Restriction League was founded by a group of Boston lawyers, professors, and wealthy philanthropists who had became upset over the hundreds of thousands of immigrants entering the United States annually. The League was especially opposed to the "new" immigrants from Southern and Eastern Europe as being "inferior beings" who were likely to become criminals or public charges if admitted to the United States.

The League decided to pursue a minimal literacy test for all immigrants as an apparently reasonable means of screening out the "new" immigrants who generally were poor and illiterate. Their efforts were to span the next two decades (see entry for 1897 and the literacy test).

May 18, 1896— The Supreme Court ruled in Plessey v. Ferguson (often known afterwards as simply the Plessey case) that segregation on the basis of "separate but equal" was Constitutional. Southern schools would use this doctrine to operate segregated school systems an in essence a segregated culture until 1954. Then, in the Brown decision, another Supreme Court would rule that "separate" is inherently unequal, and would end segregation in public schools and other public facilities.

Plessey was a black man who sued to be permitted to use any railway car rather than those set aside for blacks as Louisiana state law required. Chief Justice Brow said that although it was the clear intention of the 14th Amendment (see entry for July 28, 1868) for absolute equality for the races before the law, he ruled that "in the nature of things, it could not have been intended to abolish distinctions based upon color, or to enforce, social as distinguished from political equality, or a commingling of the two races unsatisfactorily to either."

Thus, more than 30 years after the Civil War, a Supreme Court Chief Justice was proclaiming that the 14th Amendment could not really mean what it said, because otherwise it would lead (horror of horrors) to a commingling of the races. It is easy to understand why the South maintained an officially segregated society for almost a century after the Civil War, and why elements of that society still exist today.

From an immigration standpoint, it is equally easy to understand why there was a strong negative reaction to the "swarthy" southern Italian and "dark" eastern European immigrants who began arriving in large numbers around this time. The strong West Coast bias against the "Yellow Peril" from China that became law from 1882 onward is also readily understood. Simply put, much of the United States was a highly racist society at this time, and the highest court in the country proclaimed that it was both Constitutional and desirable to be so. The restrictive immigration policies of the next half-century fitted in very well with this frame of mind.

1897 — In literally the last days of his second term of office, President Grover Cleveland, who had officiated at the dedication ceremony for the Statue of Liberty in 1886 (see entry for October 28, 1886), vetoed a bill requiring a literacy test for all immigrants. Because both houses of Congress had passed the literacy test act with relative ease in 1896, it was expected that the literacy test would readily be re-enacted in future sessions of Congress. It was in fact re-enacted, but it was vetoed by a succession of Presidents. It was not until 20 years later, in 1917, that the literacy test would become law. And even in 1917 it would require the overriding of another presidential veto by President Wilson before final passage.

The literacy test was an interesting case in the development of immigration politics. On its face, the literacy test was simple enough. A potential immigrant had to be able to read 40 words in any language, not necessarily English. The stated intent of the test was to ensure the immigrant had had enough basic schooling to be literate and therefore be able to quickly assimilate readily in the culture of the United States. Objectively, many people thought the literacy law was a reasonable and even desirable part of the screening process. Their representatives in Congress agreed. However, as is common in politics, there was more to the legislation than met the eye, and the literacy law developed powerful opposition over the next few decades.

The bill to implement the law was initially introduced in Congress in 1891 by then–Representative Henry Cabot Lodge of Massachusetts. Later, as a Senator, Lodge became essentially the spokesman for the activities of the "Immigration Restriction League" (see entry for 1894), a small but powerful group of upper class Bostonians, who were reluctantly willing to accept (partially) Irish-Americans as "honorary Anglo-Saxons," but were strongly opposed to the "new" immigrants from southern and eastern Europe. Their opposition was based on race, religion, "swarthy" looks, and generally undesirable ethnicity. The League was a strong advocate of immigration restrictions for the next two decades.

The League decided opposition to immigration on such blatant grounds as race and religion was not palatable with most people, but the League also realized that the innocent-sounding literacy test would serve their purposes of weeding out many of the new immigrants who were desperately poor and illiterate. The League pressured Henry Cabot Lodge to again introduce the literacy test bill in Congress, where, as noted before, it was generally well received as a reasonable step in the immigration process.

However, business interests as represented by the National Association of Manufacturers (NAM) were strongly opposed to immigration restrictions of any sort that could possibly reduce their source of cheap labor. Businessmen with any ties to steamship companies, now operating generally larger and faster ships, also wanted no restrictions to what had become a profitable trade in human immigrant cargo (many companies had operatives on land in many European countries drumming up immigration business). And immigrants themselves, as they became eligible to vote, were strongly opposed to immigration restrictions of any sort.

The result was a creation of voting blocs opposed to immigration restriction, and all politicians are very sensitive to voting blocs of any sorts. The literacy test became a political football. By narrow margins, Congress defeated literacy test bills in 1898, 1902, and 1906. Subsequent bills passed in 1913 and 1915, but were vetoed by Presidents Taft and Wilson in sequence. However, when Congress passed the next literacy test bill in 1917, Congress overrode Wilson's next veto and the literacy test became law.

By 1917, several restrictive immigration bills had been passed or were in process. World War I had created a very negative attitude towards immigration, and great restrictions would soon be placed on immigration. About 14.5 million additional immigrants poured into the United States in the two decades between 1900 and 1920, and there was majority agreement that it was time to call a halt. The National Origins Act of 1924 (see entry for May 26, 1924) was the final step in doing exactly that.

January 1, 1898 — By far the largest consolidation in absolute terms in American history took place when New York City (then the largest city in the nation), Brooklyn (then the fourth largest city), Queens, Staten Island, and what is now known as the Bronx, merged together (the largest consolidation in percentage terms took place in Philadelphia in 1854). The city of New York grew from 44 square miles to 299 square miles, and the 1890 population of 1.5 million grew to 3.5 million in 1900.

The explosive growth of New York City of course was only on paper in the sense that all of the combined citizens existed before the merger. However, the increase in size of the city meant that even more immigrants tended to stay within the new city boundaries and find employment in the newly enlarged city. At the end of the 19th century, two-thirds of American urban residents were still tenants rather than homeowners, and most of these renters were living in tenements of some sort is some city or another. The intense crowding in these tenements in New York City led to the new Tenement House Act of 1901 (see entry for April 12, 1901).

April 24, 1898— The United States declared war on Spain. The cause of the war was the tensions that had simmered since the battleship *Maine* was blown up in Havana, Cuba, with a loss of 260 lives on February 15. Spain was publicly blamed for the incident, but Cuba was in another fight for its independence from Spain, and many people in the United States were pushing for "Manifest Destiny" and a continuation of the 19th century expansion of the United States. These groups supported the new Cuban battle for independence. Thus, a wide variety of people with a wide variety of agendas could have been involved in the sinking of the Maine.

The Spanish fleet in the Philippines (the Philippines had also been fighting for independence from Spain) was destroyed by the United States on May 1st, and by December 10 Spain had ceded the Philippines, Puerto Rico, and Guam to the United States, and approved independence for Cuba. Along with its annexation of Hawaii on July 7, the United States suddenly had acquired an overseas "empire." Governmental issues quickly arose, and eventually related immigration issues arose as well.

The official peace treaty ending the Spanish-American war was signed February 10, 1899, but the Philippines were greatly dismayed to find they had only exchanged domination by one foreign power for another. Their battle with Spain for independence now became a battle with the United States for independence, as President McKinley declared that the people of the Philippines were too "uncivilized" to govern themselves. The resulting Philippine Insurrection did not end until 1902, and in some ways lingered on into 1905. Various immigration and other issues continued through the rest of the 1900s until the Philippines gained independence after World War II. The prime steps in that direction took place in August of 1916 with the Philippines Autonomy Act (see entry for August 29, 1916), and then in 1934 with the Tydings-McDuffie Act (see entry for March 24, 1934). Until 1934, the Filipino people were United States "nationals," with a relative ease of immigration to the United States. But once they were set on the road to independence in 1934, Filipinos became aliens, subject to the immigration laws and quotas of the time. As Asians, their immigration path became much more difficult until the changes during and after World War II.

After years of struggle, Puerto Rico had gained an autonomous government from Spain in 1897, but autonomy was very short-lived. Puerto

Rico was ceded to the United States, after the Spanish-American War. However, under the Foraker Act of 1900 (see entry for April 2, 1900) and then the Jones-Shafroth Act of 1917 (see entry for March 2, 1917), Puerto Ricans were first nationals in 1900 and then full-fledged citizens of the United States in 1917. Thus, the movement of Puerto Ricans back and forth to the mainland of the United States was one of migration rather than immigration. But some Puerto Ricans still pressed for a different status with the United States into the 21st Century as listed in several places in the rest of this chronology.

Cuba did gain a relatively independent status a few years after the Spanish-American War, but there were resentments by the Cubans about some issues they felt violated their sovereignty. Cubans immigrated to the United States on a small but regular basis during the first half on the 1900s, but the assumption of Fidel Castro to power in 1959 eventually provoked a number of immigration crises through the rest of the 1900s. Cubans fled Castro's new Communist regime, and the United States gave them special status for fleeing a Communist state only 90 miles from Florida. Then the chaotic Mariel boatlift of 1980 (see entry for March 28, 1980) brought over 125,000 Cubans to the United States and continued the antagonistic relationship between Castro and the United States in which many potential Cuban immigrants were caught in the middle.

Hawaii played no part in the Spanish-American War, except perhaps to make the United States even more aware of its strategic position in the Pacific Ocean. But as part of the emerging American empire, it was annexed in 1898 as a new American territory. The so-called Organic Act of 1900 declared that all citizens of the Republic of Hawaii as of August 12, 1898, were now citizens of the United States as well as citizens of the Territory of Hawaii.

The population of Hawaii at the time was slightly more than 150,000, over half of which were Japanese and about one-quarter Chinese. Few Japanese or Chinese were citizens of Hawaii, but per the 14th Amendment, everyone born in Hawaii after the annexation was a birthright citizen of the United States. Thus, in spite of the anti–Asian discrimination of the time, the United States would soon have tens of thousands of Asian citizens. This was an unintended consequence of the annexation, unexpected consequences being a historically common event when Congress tinkered in any way with the immigration laws, but the anti–Asian discrimination kept Hawaii from achieving statehood until 1959 (after trying at least 18 times after 1903).

The citizens of Guam, the last piece of the American Empire of 1898, remained as nationals until becoming citizens of the United States in 1950. Thus, the American Empire of 1898 involved four island nations, all with different ethnic groups, with all being treated in different ways at the time relative to rules of governance and the resulting laws of immigration. Nothing was ever simple when it came to immigration to the United States after 1898.

April 2, 1900— The Foraker Act ended military rule by the United States in Puerto Rico. The inhabitants of Puerto Rico were not yet American citizens, but they enjoyed a favorable trade and tax status, and adopted United States currency. The United States government appointed their governor, but the island had its own two-chamber legislature and other aspects similar to those of other states in the United States. The act was named after its sponsor, Ohio senator Joseph B. Foraker. The next change in status in Puerto Rico came with the Jones-Shafroth Act in 1917 (see entry for March 2, 1917).

April 12, 1901— The Tenement House Act of 1901 brought new changes to the building of tenements in New York City (and elsewhere, after being widely copied, as previous laws of New York City had been — see entry for 1867 — Tenements). The new act required indoor plumbing, with one toilet for every two families (usually 20 families occupied one five-story building with four apartments and thus four families per floor). The act also improved natural lighting conditions within the building; essentially outlawed any more tenements being built on 25-foot wide lots; and mandated changes to already existing tenements. The 1901 law became known as "the new law" and a Tenement House Commission was established to survey conditions in the city's tenements and ensure that the laws were being appropriately applied.

Landlords objected vigorously to the 1901 law, especially the part requiring indoor plumbing. They went to court, lost at the state level in 1904, and eventually lost in the United States Supreme Court in 1906. The tenements were still small and very crowded, but now they had minimally acceptable levels of sanitation and ventilation. Battles between tenants and landlords would go on through the rest of the century, and in New York City, which had more tenements than anywhere else, these battles would go on through "rent strikes" and rent control issues of higher or lower intensity in a seemingly endless procession.

September 6, 1901— A Polish anarchist named Leon Czolgosz shot President William McKinley in Buffalo, New York. McKinley died a week later on September 14, and Congress went on to pass the Anarchist Exclusion Act which barred the entrance into the United States of people judged to be anarchists and political extremists.

1902— The Chinese Exclusion Act (see entry for May 6, 1882) was again renewed, but this time there was no 10 year extension. The act was now officially in force for an indefinite period. It would not be modified unit 1943, when a nominal number of 105 Chinese immigrants were allowed to enter the United States annually in recognition of the fact that in 1943 China and the United States were now allies in World War II.

1906— The Naturalization Act of 1906 standardized certain naturalization procedures, and made some knowledge of the English language a requirement for citizenship. The act also established the Bureau of Immigration and Naturalization in the Commerce Department.

1907— The Expatriation Act was passed. This act declared that an American woman who marries a foreign national automatically loses her citizenship.

Winter 1907— The Japanese Government and the United States signed a "Gentlemen's Agreement" (on which talks continued into 1908). There was no specific single document, but rather a series of six diplomatic notes exchanged between Japan and the United States between late 1907 and early 1908. The essence of the Agreement was that the Japanese government would agree to deny passports to Japanese laborers wishing to enter the United States in exchange for a promise that the United States would not apply the Exclusion Act of 1882 (see entry for May 6, 1882) to Japanese citizens (by now, Japanese citizens constituted the largest bloc of Asian immigrants within the United States). The United States also agreed to crack down on general discrimination against Japanese-Americans, nearly all of whom lived on the West Coast.

This Agreement was meant to mollify West Coast interests who continued to rail against immigrants of all types from Asia, while seeking an accommodation with the government of Japan, which was seen as a military power by Washington. China, in contrast, was seen as weak and ineffectual. The Japanese government also wanted to preserve the image of Japan in the world and avoid the negative image a total exclusion similar to the Chinese exclusion would bring.

But the United States would break its word to the Japanese in the Immigration Act of 1924 (see entry for May 26, 1924) which would essentially bar all Asian immigrants. The Japanese were outraged and added this duplicity to the list of growing complaints that would ultimately lead to World War II.

December 31, 1907 — The year 1907 saw the highest number of new immigrant arrivals in the history of the United States at 1.285 million. The number of immigrants added to the rolls in 1990 and 1991 were 1.536 and 1.827 million respectively, but the majority of the 1990 and 1991 additions were previously illegal immigrants who had been grantee amnesty. Most had already been in the United States for a number of years. Thus, the record for the number of new immigrants actually arriving in the United States legally in one year still is held by the wave of new immigrants that came in 1907.

This means that the peak of "new" immigrants (immigrants from southern and eastern Europe) arriving in the United States before 1930 came in 1907, whereas the peak of "old" immigrants (those from northern and western Europe) came in 1882 (see entry for December 31, 1882). The arrival of more new than old immigrants first occurred in 1896. The 1882 peak of old immigrants consisted of 87 percent old immigrants and 13 percent new, while the 1907 peak of new immigrants consisted of 81 percent new immigrants and 19 percent old.

It was this majority of new southern and eastern European immigrants, led by a majority of immigrants from Italy (at its peak two million immigrants from Italy arrived between 1910 and 1920), that were seen as less desirable than the old immigrants. The new immigrants were thought of as "swarthy," illiterate, and less ambitious than the old immigrants, and the new immigrants were made up mainly of Catholics with a strong mix of Jews, and this was also seen as undesirable by the powers that be in the United States at the time.

This animosity led to the establishment of the United States Immigration Commission, know popularly as the Dillingham Commission after the name of its chairman and prime mover, Senator William P. Dillingham, to study the immigration issue. This Commission was made up of nine members, three each being appointed by the president, the speaker of the house, and the president pro tem of the Senate. The Dillingham Commission conducted the first large-scale study of immigration ever sponsored by the Government of the United States. The commission was in existence between 1907 and 1910, and published its report (highly critical of the "new" immigration) in 1911 (see entry for 1911–Dillingham). The report would lead to strong restrictions on immigration in the coming years.

January 1910— The Angel Island immigration facility in San Francisco Bay became operational. In a sense Angel Island was the West Coast equivalent of Ellis Island in New York Harbor (see entry for January 1, 1892), but in its lifetime of 30 years Angel Island processed at most 300,000 immigrants (nearly all Asian), while Ellis Island processed about 12 million of all types. So the two facilities were hardly equal except in the sense that they both processed immigrants under the direction of the federal government. Also, while the Ellis Island experience became part of a fond memory for the immigrants who were processed there, Angel Island was remembered as part of an ugly memory for most immigrants processed there.

The basic purpose of Angel Island was to continue to implement the Chinese Exclusion Act of 1882 (see entry for May 6, 1882). Initially the act had been implemented by local customs service officers on an individual and somewhat arbitrary basis. Then the responsibility was picked up by the then Immigration and Naturalization Service (INS) created in 1891 (see entry for 1891) which attempted to standardize Immigration procedures. Angel Island became one of the facilities on the West Coast for this purpose, but because its function was primarily one of enforcement and it function mainly as a detention center, Angel Island became infamous as a place of fear and loathing by the immigrants it processed.

Angel Island replaced an old two-story shed on the Pacific Mail Steamship Company wharf in San Francisco, which had been used to process immigrants previously. But better amenities were not the basic purpose of Angel Island. The island was the largest in the Bay, but it was well removed from the mainland, and thus well isolated and essentially escape-proof. European or other travelers arriving by ship and holding first or second class tickets would be processed on board and allowed to disembark. Remaining immigrants would be diverted to Angel Island for processing.

The prime strategy of the Chinese processed at Angel Island was to try to find entrance to the United States via an exception to the Chinese Exclusion Act. Many would buy false documents so they could claim to be children of exempt classes such as merchants, clergy, diplomats, teachers, and students. Children born of Chinese nationals, here or abroad, were also exempt. The disastrous San Francisco earthquake of 1906, in which many municipal records, including birth certificates, were destroyed, actually gave many Chinese the opportunity to claim to be children of Chinese who had become citizens by virtue of birth in this country or by virtue of birth to Chinese who were citizens and had children while traveling abroad.

The Chinese who tried this ploy were known as "paper sons" (or less frequently "paper daughters") had to survive intensive interrogation by a Board of Special Inquiry and memorize lists of facts only such children would know. The lists of facts were available for sale just as other documents providing "proof" of a claim of exemption were. There could be long waits of months on Angel Island while the "facts" were checked. But then, as now, the desire to enter the United States was strong enough to overcome many difficulties. Many of the Chinese who passed the interrogations were, of course, "illegal immigrants." But also, as today, many people gladly took whatever steps were necessary to enter the United States.

For Japanese immigrants already in the country, who at the time were not subject to specific exclusion laws except the Gentlemen's Agreement of 1907 (see entry for Winter 1907), Angel Island was the place of happier memories because between 6,000 and 19,000 "picture brides" were processed through Angel Island by 1920. Picture brides agreed to be married to Japanese men in the United States through the process of sending pictures (and

1911

other communications) to the Japanese men and saving the prohibitive costs of actual trips back to and from the United States and Japan.

Overall, it was estimated that from 11 to 30 percent of all immigrants arriving at Angel Island were ultimately deported. This compared to a rate of from one to two percent at Ellis Island. The difference was to be expected as Angel Island was primarily meant to be a screening facility to find potential deportees while Ellis Island was more of a welcoming facility.

1911—Dillingham—The Dillingham Commission (see entry for December 31, 1907) published a 42-volume report after three years of study and hearings. The data contained in the report would eventually become a treasure trove for historians, but the conclusions contained in the report, often based on misuse or misinterpretations of the data, would ultimately be devastating to potential new immigrants. New immigration laws in 1917, 1921, and 1924 (see entries for February 5, 1917, May 1921, and May 26, 1924) would ultimately flow from the report.

The Dillingham Report warned that the "new" immigration from southern and eastern Europe threatened to subvert American society. The report identified the genetic makeup of the new immigrants as a major problem, and proposed that quotas be established to limit the number of certain national groups permitted to enter the United States. The beginning of World War I in Europe slowed the generation of new laws implementing these ideas, but they came to fruition starting in 1917.

1911—Eugenics—The president of the Immigration Restriction League (see entry for 1894) Prescott Hall asked a former Harvard classmate, Charles Davenport, for assistance in determining methods to influence the ongoing Congressional debate about immigration. Hall and his League wanted to insure that future immigration laws would become more restrictive.

Charles Davenport was involved with the Eugenics Record Office (ERO). Eugenics was at the time was a popular phenomena which led to some truly ugly episodes in the first half of the 1900s. It had been developed as a "science" which postulated that the gene pool of the human race (the white part) was being deteriorated because non-desirables (non-whites) were breeding faster than whites. The book entitled *The Rising Tide of Color Against White World Supremacy* by Lothrop Stoddard gives an idea of the frankly racist quality of the eugenics movement. But many famous people supported the movement as a way to improve the "quality" of the human race in the future. Nearly all of these were ultimately highly embarrassed to have been supporters of the movement at one time when it was finally fully revealed as a pseudo-science.

At any rate, eugenics was popular at the time, and its tenets fitted in well with those who wanted to restrict immigration, especially that from southern and eastern Europeans. Charles Davenport recommended a survey to determine the national origins of "hereditary defectives" in American prisons, mental hospitals, and other charitable institutions. Davenport appointed his ERO colleague Harry Laughlin to manage the program. This essentially assured the survey would find what they were looking for, and the results could be used to try to influence Congress to pass restrict immigration legislation. Laughlin would appear before a house committee writing such legislation in 1920 (see entry for 1920) and be appointed an expert eugenics agent by the chairman of the committee. There was no doubt that the fraudulent science of eugenics played a significant part in the writing of immigration laws in the 1900–29 period. Their effect would not be overcome until the dramatic changes of 1965 (see entry for October 2, 1965).

1913— California implemented an Alien Land Law prohibiting aliens ineligible for citizenship (Chinese and Japanese) from owning property in the state. It was another example of strong anti–Asian discrimination in California, but it served as a model for similar anti–Asian laws in other states.

1913 — INS— As immigration administration became more important with a greatly increased number of immigrants, the Bureau of Immigration and Naturalization was moved to the newly separated Department of Labor, and the Bureau was divided into a Bureau of Immigration and a Bureau of Naturalization, each with its own Commissioner.

1914— The Public Health Service (PHS), whose duties included medical examination of immigrants disembarking at Ellis Island, also accepted eugenic "theory" in turning back "inferior stock" as represented by "new" immigrants. The Surgeon General, who headed the PHS, and a number of his senior officers, became publicly aligned with the eugenics movement, taking key positions in eugenic organizations and publishing articles of support. The fact that the PHS so prominently supported what was the bogus science of eugenics gave great credence to those who supported more restrictive immigration laws.

August 1, 1914— Marcus Garvey, a Jamaica-born black nationalist, founded the Universal Negro Improvement Association (UNIA). He urged blacks to plan to return to Africa where they could find true freedom, and in 1919 he founded the Black Star Line for the purpose of providing transportation to Africa for those blacks who wished to return. He re-energized the concept of blacks finding freedom by emigrating to the land from which their slave ancestors had been forcibly removed.

But Garvey was unable to convince Liberia, the African nation founded by free blacks in the 1800s (see entry for December 1816) to grant land for new black emigrants from the United States to settle. Further, his Black Star Line failed, and Garvey spent time in prison for mail fraud in connection with questionable stock sales of the company. He was later deported to Jamaica, and then moved to London in 1935, where he died in 1940 at the age of 53. His "return to Africa" movement (which later identified Ethiopia as the "land of our fathers") never came to fruition and essentially faded away.

However, Garvey was remembered among blacks for his eloquent speeches urging black pride and self-sufficiency. He established a number of black organizations and businesses in the United States before he was sent to prison, and he was recognized as an inspirational figure in the Civil Rights movement of the 1960s. In 1964 his body was returned from London to Jamaica where he was declared the country's first national hero.

August 4, 1914— President Woodrow Wilson proclaimed neutrality for the United States in the European War that would become World War I. Immigration during the war would not decline as much as might have been expected (immigration from 1910-1919 was 6.3 million, reaching the second highest level for any prior decade, and higher than any decade before 1900), but the attitude towards immigration underwent a dramatic change.

The attitude towards German immigrants, the largest group of immigrants received by the United States to date, turned negative as the War progressed and the body counts in Europe increased. When the British ship *Lusitania* was sunk in 1915 by the Germans with a loss of 128 American passengers, anti–German feelings steadily increased until the United States entered the War in 1917 (see entry for April 6, 1917).

But there was a growing feeling in the United States that had the sense of "a plague upon both of your houses." The attitude was that the fabled high civilization of Europe was a joke and that the real state of affairs there was one of constant wars over the centuries. The supposedly sophisticated Europeans were actually a bunch of savages, and immigration from Europe was no longer a thing to be desired. A sense of isolationism was settling in and would become the major trend towards immigration when the war ended. In addition, an intense dislike for anything to do with Communism which had overtaken Russia during the war would harden attitudes towards immigrants (and existing citizens) who seemed to be, or had been, or might be involved with communism in any way.

1916—Carl Brigham, who a decade later would lay the groundwork for what became the Scholastic Aptitude Test (SAT), took part in a series of "intelligence" tests at the request of the Army to better match recruits with assignments in the military. Brigham wrote a book *A Study of American Intelligence* based on the test results. The book was used by various groups to advance agendas not necessarily agreed to by Brigham, who was a serious educator who went on to a career filled with various breakthroughs in the field of education.

Brigham had broken down his test results analytically by race. He wrote that American education was declining and would continue to do as the "racial mixture" in schools became more extensive (schools at the time were still reflecting the effects of segregation). He also cited the supposed low quality of recruits of southern and eastern European heritage. Various anti-immigration groups took this citing as more reason to restrict immigration from those areas, and this reasoning played a big role in the restrictive immigration laws written in the next year and through the next decade. Further, supporters of the since fully discredited "science" of eugenics joined the clamor for more restrictive immigration laws.

August 29, 1916—The Philippines Autonomy Act was signed by President Wilson after a long battle in the Congress to agree on the language

1917

of the act. The prime sponsor of the act was William Atkinson Jones (who also later sponsored the Jones-Shafroth Act in 1917 for Puerto Rico citizenship — see entry for March 2, 1917). Representative Jones first sponsored a bill in 1912 to give the Philippines independence on July 4, 1921. But the bill could not get further than approval by his House committee.

Jones tried again in 1914, and a bill was finally passed by 1916 giving the Philippines independence "as soon as a stable government can be established therein." The bill did create an all–Philippine legislature, and some other improved autonomy issues. The declaration of a fixed date for the Philippines had to wait until the Tydings-McDuffie Act of 1934 (see entry for March 24, 1934). Then immigration issues related to residents of an independent nation (aliens) versus residents of a territory of the United States (nationals) would take the shine off independence for some Filipinos.

February 5, 1917 — Congress overrode the Veto of President Woodrow Wilson and passed the Immigration Act of 1917 (also known as the Asiatic Barred Zone Act). The 1917 act contained the literacy test requirement for immigrants Congress had been pursuing for twenty years (see entry for 1897). More dramatically, the 1917 bill also designated an "Asiatic Barred Zone," a geographical region including much of Eastern Asia and specific Pacific Islands from which immigrants would not be admitted to the United States. Essentially only Japan and the Philippines would be eligible for immigration from Asia. Also excluded were immigrants unable to meet certain mental, physical, economic, and moral standards, as well as political standards such as not being suspected of being anarchists. The act tried to be as inclusive as possible in barring what were considered undesirables. It specifically barred idiots, feeble-minded persons, epileptics, insane persons, alcoholics, professional beggars, all persons mentally or physically defective, polygamists, and anarchists.

The Act of 1917 continued what had become standard immigration practice in the early 1900s in that certain restrictions in immigration law were continued if not reinforced in subsequent revisions of the law. The legislature of the United States was now committed to the placement of restrictions on immigration. Many of the restrictions grew out of the Dillingham Commission Report in 1911 (see entry for 1911–Dillingham) as supported by members of the eugenics movement (see entry for 1911–Eugenics).

March 2, 1917— The Jones-Shafroth Act was signed by President Wilson, granting United States citizenship to Puerto Ricans, making the island a territory of the United States. Puerto Ricans could not vote in elections in the United States, but they were represented by a Commissioner (also non-voting) in the House of Representatives. The act also specified that male Puerto Ricans were eligible for the draft now going on to prepare the military of the United States for its new role in World War I.

There was a perception at the time by many that citizenship was granted in exchange for Puerto Ricans becoming eligible for the draft, but the Jones-Shafroth Act was in the planning stage long before World War I involved the United States (Representative Jones had already sponsored an independence act for the Philippines — see entry for August 29, 1916). In addition, being considered as permanent residents of the United States made male Puerto Ricans susceptible to the draft whether or not they were citizens.

As citizens of the United States, many Puerto Ricans moved to the "mainland" to find better economic opportunities, as many "conventional" immigrants from other countries had done before them. However, the Puerto Ricans were not subject to the tightening immigration restrictions of the time because they were citizens, not immigrants. Many moved to the New York City area because of its availability of jobs and the relative ease of transportation to go there.

Many Puerto Ricans were also recruited to Connecticut to harvest fruits and pick Tobacco. They suffered much discrimination and exploitation as many immigrants do, even though the Puerto Ricans were United States citizens. Improvements in the ease and costs of transportation as the 1900s wore on made it easier for Puerto Ricans to move between their island and the northeast United States, centered on the New York City area, as economic conditions changed. In many places Puerto Ricans are still treated as undesirable immigrants, even though they are actually citizens and have the same rights to live and work anywhere as any other citizens do. Puerto Rico would be granted Commonwealth status in 1952 (see entry for July 25, 1952), which resulted in greater autonomy, but did not change the fact of already existing citizenship for all Puerto Ricans.

April 6, 1917— The United States declared war with Germany, and by June 26 troops from the United States arrived in Europe. There was a

burst of patriotism and bond drives to fund the war were extremely successful. But the preparations for the war were intermixed with a flu epidemic
that would eventually kill an estimated 20 million people worldwide, including about 550,000 in the United States. It was part of an almost bittersweet
feeling that would evolve from the war despite the initial enthusiasm, and
leave a negative attitude towards immigration that had been growing since
the start of the war in Europe in 1914 (see entry for August 4, 1914).

November 11, 1918 — On the "eleventh hour of the eleventh day of the
eleventh month," an armistice would take effect to end World War I. Peace
negotiations into the following year would find President Wilson stricken
with the omnipresent flu and unable to pursue the details of the peace he
wanted. Historians agree that the punitive peace that did occur simply set
the stage for World War II two decades later. Anti-immigration efforts continued to grow in the Unite States, especially toward previous or new
immigrants who might be suspected of communistic sympathies.

June 2, 1919 — Several bombs were detonated in eight American cities,
including one in Washington, D.C., that damaged the home of newly
appointed Attorney General A. Mitchell Palmer (and nearly injured future
President Franklin Roosevelt, then in the Navy Department who lived
across the street and was out walking with his wife). The bombs were
placed by Gallenist anarchists (followers of Luigi Gallenai) who left flyers
clearly indicating the bombings were part of their attempt to overthrow
the government of the United States by force.

Gallenai and several followers (excluding the bomber of the attorney
general's house, Carlo Valdonoci, who was killed when the bomb went off
prematurely and blew up in his face as he was placing it at the house) were
deported three weeks later as resident aliens who had advocated the violent overthrow of the government. The deportations marked the beginning of intense activity to arrest and deport other anarchists, communists,
and similar persons identified as dangerous to the United States.

The battle actually had been going on since early in since 1915 when
President Wilson warned of "hyphenated Americans" who have poured the
poison of disloyalty into American life and must be crushed. By 1917 Congress had passed the Espionage Act which was followed by the Sedition

Act of 1918, both aimed at radicals who encouraged men to refuse the draft for World War I and to desert if they were already enlisted. The events of June 1919 brought things to a head.

The Bureau of Investigation of the Justice Department (the forerunner of the FBI) under J. Edgar Hoover (who would spend almost the next half century tracking down communists), was operating under greatly increased funds approved by Congress. Considerable information was gathered on radicals Emma Goldman (who had an index of 10,000 names) and Alexander Berkman in various raids. The information was used to deport 249 radicals of Russian origin to Russia on December 21, 1919, via the ship *Buford*, (called the Red Ark or the Russian Ark by journalists). Emma Goldman and Alexander Berkman were aboard.

The raids, known as the Palmer Raids, continued into 1920. Ultimately between four and six thousand people were arrested (some put the total at 10,000). About 500 were deported. There were many outcries about violations of due process and civil rights, but generally the public was behind what became known as the raids of the "Red Scare." From an immigration standpoint, the Red Scare put Congress under increasing pressure to curb immigration from all sources. The restrictive laws of the time and the 1920s were greatly influenced by the events of the Palmer Raids.

1920— Harry Laughlin (see entry for 1911–Eugenics) was called upon by the House of Representatives Committee on Immigration and Naturalization as a witness. Laughlin presented the data he had been accumulating for almost a decade, and he took the position that the data confirmed the American gene pool was being polluted by the increasing number of southern and eastern European immigrants. He claimed such immigrants to be both intellectually and morally defective.

The Committee was sympathetic to Laughlin's testimony, and Chairman Albert Johnson of the state of Washington appointed Laughlin as an "expert eugenics agent" whose testimony would be useful in further actions of Congress on immigration. In this capacity, Laughlin conducted additional research from 1921 to 1931, having his results published by the Government Printing Office. He testified on the 1924 Immigration Restriction Act (see entry for May 26, 1924) and urged that an eugenics-crafted bill be implemented (which in many respects it was).

1921

The Eugenics Research Association displayed a chart beneath the Rotunda of the Capitol building in Washington showing the costs to taxpayers of supporting those Laughlin had described as "social inadequates." The eugenics issue heavily permeated the atmosphere in Washington during the decade of the 1920s when new immigration laws were being implemented in 1921, 1924, and 1929 (see entries for May 1921, May 26, 1924, and 1929).

May 1921— A quota system was established for immigrants under the Emergency Quota Act. The "emergency" was because the act superseded a prior proposal in the House to simply stop immigration for a year on an emergency basis to slow down the flood of immigrants while a more permanent solution was worked out. But William P. Dillingham was still in the Senate and he took the opportunity to re-introduce the quota system he had proposed following the publication of the Dillingham report in 1911 (see entry for 1911–Dillingham) before World War I and delayed implementation of his suggestions. The 1921 act was also known as the Johnson Quota Act after Albert W. Johnson, one its prime proponents in Congress.

The Congress decided to go along with the suggested quota system for a year, but it was renewed two more times until the more restrictive law of 1924 was developed (see entry for May 26, 1924). Under the 1921 system, the number of immigrants admitted to the United States from any nation for each year could not exceed three percent of the number of foreign-born residents from that nation living in the United States as of the census of 1910. There were certain exceptions, but the thrust of the law was to restrict further the number and kind of immigrants entering the United States.

A statement by Albert Johnson, who also was the Chairman of the Immigration and Naturalization in the House of Representatives at the time, accurately summed up the Isolationist attitude in Congress in this period: "The United States of America, a nation great in all things, is ours today. To whom will it belong tomorrow...? The United States is our land. If it was not the land of our fathers, at least it may be, and it should be, the land of our children. We intend to maintain it so. The day of unalloyed welcome to all people, the day of indiscriminate acceptance of all races, has definitely ended."

1922— The Cable Act (formally known as the Married Woman's Independent Nationality Act) partially repealed the Expatriation Act (see entry for 1907) that had mandated that any woman marrying a foreign national loses her citizenship. Under the Cable Act a woman marrying a foreign national and staying within the United States could retain her citizenship. However, if she married a foreign national and lived abroad for as much as two years, she could still lose her right to American nationality. Further, any woman who married an Asian (or anyone ineligible for citizenship) still automatically lost her citizenship.

1923— The Supreme Court ruled that Indians (from the country of India on the Asian subcontinent) cannot become citizens of the United States. The case, entitled the United States vs. Bhaghat Singh Thind, was considered a landmark decision codifying the discriminatory intent of present immigration laws against Asians.

May 26, 1924— The Immigration Act of 1924, known as The National Origins Act (or the Reed-Johnson Act), reduced the quotas set in 1921 (see entry for May 1921) for those immigrants deemed to be less desirable for entry into the United States. The quotas were reduced to two percent (from three percent) of the number of foreign nationals living in the United States as of 1890 (rather than 1910). Because far fewer residents from southern and eastern Europe were living in the United States in 1890 than in 1910, the new quotas represented a dramatic reduction in the permitted number of immigrants from southern and eastern Europe. The quota essentially fell from 45 percent to 15 percent.

However, the quotas for those from northern and western Europe were relatively generous because there were large numbers of such immigrants in the United States in 1890, and requests for immigration from those areas had been declining. Immigration from other parts of the world was almost all cut back on the same basis as that from Southern and Eastern Europe.

The two-percent rule was to be phased out on July 1, 1927, and replaced by an overall cap of 150,000 immigrants annually, with quotas to be determined by "national origins" as of the census of 1920. Initially immigration from other Americas was allowed, but measures were quickly developed to deny legal entry to Mexican laborers.

Additionally, a provision of the law barred entry to all immigrants ineligible for citizenship, thus effectively barring all Asians, including for-eign-born wives and the children of American citizens of Chinese ances-try. This provision unilaterally negated the 1907 Gentlemen's Agreement with Japan (see entry for Winter 1907) and enraged the Japanese govern-ment. May 26, the effective date of the Act, was declared a day of national humiliation in Japan, with associated protests in Tokyo. It was another item in the growing list of disagreements between Japan and the United States that would ultimately lead to World War II.

The 1924 Act was essentially the last major step in restricting immi-gration into the United States in the first half of the twentieth century. All parts of the Act did not take full effect until the end of the 1920s, so its full effect was not felt until it was combined with the beginning of the Great Depression in 1930. As President Calvin Coolidge signed the 1924 bill, he commented "America must remain American." This phrase became a rallying cry for all anti-immigration groups, especially the eugenicists. Essentially, this immigration attitude would not fully end until the huge changes brought by the Immigration and Nationality Act of 1965 (see entry for October 2, 1965).

After averaging over six million immigrants per decade in the first three decades of the 1920s, immigration totals in the 1930s fell to 0.7 mil-lion, about a tenth of the average in the previous three decades, and the smallest decade total since the 1820s. The total of the 1920s would not be matched again until the 1970s following the great liberalization of immi-gration law in 1965.

Looking back, many future groups would decry the 1924 law as the result of the extreme nativism of relatively few and some conservative Republicans. However, the law was passed just before the nominating con-ventions of both parties, and both had plenty of time to write any stren-uous objections into their platforms for the presidential elections in the fall. The Republicans endorsed the new law, and the losing Democrats, badly divided, "could only reiterate their habitual opposition to Asian immigration." By the time of the presidential election of 1928, the Democ-rats were no longer divided as their candidate, Al Smith, "the hero of the cities," said that the "laws which limit immigration must be preserved in full force and effect." As in so many cases when groups look back on his-torical legislative actions they are now ashamed of, a "radical fringe" is blamed. But the truth is, as it was in the 1920s, the majority of the whole nation was in favor of the legislation at the time.

1924— As part of the dramatic immigration reforms of 1924, the Border Patrol was created both to combat smuggling of all kinds and to protect against illegal immigration.

1929— Completing the immigration law changes of 1924 (see entry for May 26, 1924), the National Origins Formula began a quota that limited national immigration to a total of 150,000 annually, and completely forbade immigration of any sort from Asia. Only immigration from the Western Hemisphere was permitted, and that only within established quotas for individual nations and the overall total quota for the United States. The immigration switch was basically turned to "off."

The severe immigration restrictions of the 1920s would soon become an essentially moot issue due to the overriding difficulties of the worldwide depression of the 1930s and the lack of potential immigrants in that decade. But certain restrictions would become an issue in the cases of hopeful immigrants trying to escape with their lives from the dangers of nations ruled by ruthless dictators, such as Jews fleeing from Hitler.

1930— Congress passed an act permitting the admission of women as immigrants who were married to United States citizens before 1924 (and the restrictive immigration act of that year — see entry for May 26, 1924).

April 17, 1930— Although most people connect the beginning of the Great Depression with the stock market crash of October 1929, the stock market had regained by this date 96 percent of the value it had before the events of the infamous "Black Thursday" of October 24, 1929. Optimism abounded in Washington, D.C., and in June President Herbert Hoover would tell a delegation of clergymen who had come to ask for a public works program, "You have come 60 days too late. The depression is over."

But April 17 marked the high point for the stock market in 1930 (and the next 24 years). Economic conditions would decline relentlessly in the United States for the next two years, the stock market losing almost 90 percent of its 1929 value by July of 1932. Unemployment would reach a record high of 12 million in 1932. Immigration in the 1930s would decline to an official total of about 0.7 million, but careful research of official data would show that nearly as many people emigrated from the United States as immigrated to it, so that net immigration to the United States in that decade was only a little above zero.

In spite of the restrictive immigration laws of the 1920s, total immigration in that decade reached over 4 million. This was still the fourth highest decade on record because the last of the restrictive laws did not become fully effective until 1929 (the yearly average was cut in half after 1924). But the poor economic conditions of the 1930s make it difficult to determine how far immigration would have fallen if the new restrictive laws alone had driven down immigration in a decade of normal economic activity. The immigration level of the 1920s would not be reached again until the 1970s.

With the depression roaring around them, Presidents Hoover and Roosevelt (who was elected in November of 1932 and inaugurated in March of 1933) took basically the same attitude towards immigration. Not anxious to have more people dependent on the government, both men told the immigration department to emphasize the "LPC" clause (likely to become a public charge) of the immigration law to keep out immigrants who might require public assistance. The interpretation of the law was even broadened to keep out immigrants who did not have substantial funds on hand. This further reduced the pool of immigrants eligible for immigration to the United States. Regardless on the innovated programs to restore people to work introduced by Roosevelt (the most successful and long lasting probably being the Federal Housing Administration (FHA) which did jump start the critical housing construction industry and put even low skilled immigrants back to work), most historians agree it was the need to arm the country and create suitable armed forces for World War II that really ended the depression of the 1930s in the United States.

1933—Albert Einstein, the great theoretical physicist, escaped persecution by the Nazis by immigrating to the United States from Germany. Unfortunately, many other Jews, thinking Hitler is just a passing phenomenon, did not follow his example at a time when such immigration was still possible. Almost no one in the world at the time had any idea of the atomic bomb that would grow out of Einstein's theories, and which would play such a big part in finally ending World War II.

March 24, 1934 — The Tydings-McDuffie Act (officially known as the Philippine Independence Act) granted independence to the Philippines effective July 4, 1946 (1945 was the originally specified date but it would be delayed by one year by World War II).

However, the Act also changed the status of Filipinos from "national" to "alien." The Philippines were owned by the United States following the Spanish-American war in 1898 (see entry for April 24, 1898), and thus Filipinos could legally travel to and work within the United States as nationals. After being put on the path to independence, Filipinos as "aliens" were subject to existing immigration laws with a quota of only 50 persons per year (the quota was increased to 100 per year in 1943 when the Chinese Exclusion Act was repealed — see entry for December 17, 1943).

The revisions in the immigration law in 1952 (see entry for June 27, 1952) and the great liberalization of 1965 (see entry for October 2, 1965) would ease most of these immigration restrictions. The Philippines would become a strong source of immigrants to the United States from about the 1970s onward. But no one knew that at the time in 1934.

1935 — Public Law 162 granted citizenship to several hundred Asian military veterans who served the United States during World War I.

August 14, 1935 — As part of the huge flurry of acts introduced by the Roosevelt Administration to combat the effects of the depression, the Social Security Act was passed. Social Security became an important part of the lives of Americans in the following decades in a way that was undreamed of in 1935.

Social Security account numbers became so ubiquitous that they eventually replaced employee numbers at places of employment, and became the basic identification number for bank accounts, credit cards, and nearly every other financial transaction. Social security numbers would be obtained for children soon after birth to identify them as dependents on tax returns provided to the Internal Revenue Service (IRS). Your social security number would become your national identification number.

Accordingly, a social security number would become the key piece of identification needed by illegal immigrants to be permitted to work in the United States, and to function within the country in many other ways. An industry would be created underground to issue counterfeit social security cards, and the careless way the federal government would go about permitting the cards to be used illegally would become a great issue in the 2007 debates about a new immigration bill and its eventual rejection (see entries for June 3, 7, 14, 26 and 28, 2007). It would turn out, as with so many things related to illegal immigration), the capability existed to solve the social security card issue, but the federal government really didn't care that much, and the employers benefiting from the cheap labor of illegal immigrants were happy to pretend to be in apparent compliance with appropriate laws. The debates of 2007 appeared likely to end this "let's pretend" situation. It was a story no one could imagine in 1935.

August 2, 1939—Albert Einstein, who had emigrated to the United States in 1933 (see entry for 1933) to escape the Nazis in Germany, sent (or actually simply signed) a letter alerting President Roosevelt to the possibility of building an atomic bomb based on recent discoveries in physics and nuclear research. The process started by the letter resulted in the first nuclear chain reaction on December 2, 1942, at the University of Chicago under a group of physicists led by Enrico Fermi, an immigrant from Italy who had also earlier fled to the United States with his wife to avoid pressure from anti–Jewish factions in that country. The atomic bomb finally resulted in 1945 from the efforts of many persons, including immigrants Einstein and Fermi at the beginning of the process. Many prime contributors to the development of the atomic bomb were also Jewish, and many of those were benefactors of immigration to the United States.

1940—The Alien Registration Act required the registration and fingerprinting of all aliens in the United States over the age of 14.

1941—In a step focusing more on war than immigration per se, Congress passed an act refusing visas to foreigners whose presence in the United States might endanger public safety.

December 7, 1941—The Japanese attacked Pearl Harbor, drawing the

United States into what would become World War II. Aside from the obvious decrease in immigration resulting from worldwide hostilities, the fortunes of war would cause a dramatic shift in the countries allied with the United States and produce profound shifts in immigration policies accordingly.

At the beginning of the war, Japan was the prime enemy in Asia and China still the target of discrimination that had been going on formally since the Chinese Exclusion Act of 1882 (see entry for May 6, 1882). That changed by 1943 with the Magnuson Act (see entry for December 17, 1943) revoking the Exclusion Act of our new ally against the Japanese, China. However, when a Communist Regime took over China after the war, China became a prime adversary of the United States and Japan was hurriedly brought out of its occupational status to help serve as a bulwark against Communist China.

Similarly in Europe, our Russian allies helped defeat the prime enemy, Germany. But when Russia's communist regime took over eastern Europe after the war, Russia became the prime enemy and the United States quickly found a new ally in Germany against the Communists, as the Berlin Airlift of 1948 soon demonstrated.

The result of the war on immigration was not only the emergence of policies to deal with Displaced Persons, Refugees, and Asylum seekers in general as outlined in detail in the rest of this chronology, it was the emergence of persons fleeing any Communist controlled nation as the top preference on the immigration list. As the so-called Cold War evolved, any immigrants fleeing a Communist Regime (especially including Cubans after 1959) became a trophy of the Cold War for the United States. Such immigrants would receive special benefits and not be counted against any numerical quota. From an immigration standpoint, up to the great change in the immigration laws in 1965 (see entry for October 2, 1965), a major result of World War II would be the shift to an intense anti–Communist feeling by the United States.

Although fewer nations were involved, and a different sequence of events took place, an intensive anti–Communist feeling by the United States was also a major result of World War I from an immigration standpoint (see entry for August 4, 1914).

1942 — The rounding up of Japanese-Americans for detention began this year as a result of Japan and United States being at war following the bombing of Pearl Harbor in Hawaii on December 7, 1941 (see entry). The detention of the Japanese-Americans would become a great embarrassment for the United States after the war, but the process began amid much panic and anger following the bombing of Pearl Harbor.

1942 — bracero— The governments of the United States and Mexico agreed on what was called the "bracero" plan to bring Mexican laborers to work temporarily in the United States to essentially replace Americans going off to the military to fight in World War II. The program was originally intended to end in 1947, but there were extensions and then the Korean War in the 1950s caused the program to be modified and extended. The program did not finally end until 1964.

As an example of unintended consequences, the bracero program had much to do with the continuing flow of illegal immigrants into the United States, and it developed to an even higher level the familiarity with and depended on the cheap wages manufacturers and even individuals associated with illegal immigrants. In that way the program became an important link in the long-term encouragement of illegal immigrants to come to the United States that was abruptly ended by the era of enforcement that developed in 2007. The appendix contains a detailed discussion of the bracero program and its ultimate effects on illegal immigration.

June 1943— What became known as the "Zoot Suit" riots broke out between sailors and Mexican youths in Los Angeles. The zoot suit was the name given to wide-shouldered baggy-pants suits worn by aficionados of jazz music, especially young adult Mexicans. The riots in Los Angeles were followed two weeks later by race riots in Detroit (where an astounding 34 persons were killed and 700 injured) and by race riots in Harlem in New York on August 2nd (six persons were killed). But the riots in Detroit were basically between blacks and whites, and were the culmination of long-festering tensions between the two races as poor blacks from the south poured into Detroit in search of high-paying factory jobs in spite of segregated housing which was inadequate at best. World War II preparations brought matters to a head in 1943 as the demographic changes in workforces and cultures escalated to a riot level. Similar tensions brought about the Harlem riots.

However, the riots in Los Angeles added an immigration flavor to the World War II preparations in that Mexicans were the largest minority group in Los Angeles. Many had come illegally in the previous decade fleeing the Mexican revolution, adding to the many already there to work in the agriculture industry in California. There were also many Mexicans and other groups who had come to work in the booming defense industries in Southern California. Adding the young members of the military who were training in California before going off to war made a volatile mix when all of these groups congregated in downtown Los Angeles for a night out on the town (as many as 50,000 servicemen could concentrate in Los Angeles on a given weekend).

As is often the case, a fist fight between soldiers and sailors on leave and Mexicans in zoot suits escalated into a period of rioting in the first week of June 1943. Military men went on the prowl seeking "revenge" as their Mexican opponents did the same. The riots ended when the military officers in charge declared downtown Los Angeles "off limits" to their personnel on leave in the area.

Although there were many descriptions of violent battles and fist fights during the riots in Los Angeles, no one was reported killed. Observers felt that the lack of deaths in the Los Angeles riots (as compared to the 34 deaths in Detroit, for example) was due to the fact that the combatants in Los Angeles, servicemen and Mexican youths, were largely transitory populations whose members at any given time were in transit to their next location. In Detroit, the black and white combatants had been in conflict for some time and there were many events that were felt deserving of "retaliation" when the riots finally broke out.

December 17, 1943— The first small symbolic step in reversing the restrictive immigration laws of the first part of the twentieth century came when Congress passed the Magnuson Act repealing the Chinese Exclusion Act of 1882 (see entry for May 6, 1882). The Magnuson act allowed 105 Chinese immigrants to enter the United States annually per the existing quotas set in 1924 (see entry for May 26, 1924). China was now an ally of the United States in World War II, and the old Chinese Exclusion Act was seen as being hopelessly outdated. The quota of 105 Chinese immigrants annually was extremely small, but it was seen as the beginning of a new era.

Further, the act permitted Chinese nationals already residing in the United States to become naturalized citizens. This marked the first time since the Naturalization Act of 1790 that Asians were permitted to be naturalized.

The husband of famous Chinese author Pearl S. Buck was a New York publisher and he played an active role in getting the Exclusion Act repealed. Further, the bombing of Pearl Harbor by the Japanese and their brutal war against China had swung public opinion against Japan and in favor of China and China's elegant spokeswoman, Madame Chiang Kai-shek. President Roosevelt supported the new status for China by saying that, "while it would give the Chinese a preferred status over certain other Oriental people, their great contribution to the cause of decency and freedom entitles them to such preference."

August 21, 1944— Representatives of the United States and other major powers met at Dumbarton Oaks in Washington, D.C., to begin a meeting that took seven weeks to work out the formation of a postwar world organization that became the United Nations. The United States, of course, would become an active and persuasive member of the organization.

The activities of the United Nations in the immediate postwar period would focus strongly on the fate of displaced persons and other refugees around the world. The United States, as a signatory member, would agree to follow the recommendations of the United Nations on these issues, and would permit many of these recommendations relative to immigration to override the existing immigration laws in the United States. For this reason, individual laws would be passed in Congress (as noted afterwards in this Chronology) to accommodate the commitments of the United States to the United Nations. These actions helped to eliminate some racist elements of the immigration laws being carried over from the earlier years of the twentieth century.

September 2, 1945— The official end of World War II marked the beginning of the shift in alliances and immigration implications described in the entry for December 7, 1941. During 1945, a federal law, known as the War Brides Act, authorized the admission to the United States without regard to existing quotas or other issues of wives and children of citizens of the United States who had served in the armed forces during the war. The act would later be applied to the Korean War, which started in 1950.

Also, during 1945, Congress agreed to the United Nations Participation Act. This act dealt with the process by which the United States joined the newly created United Nations (see entry for August 21, 1944) and included agreeing to immigration issues specified by the United Nations, which were to be conducted in a fair and non-discriminatory manner.

The end of the war resulted in Congress classifying people fleeing the effects of Nazi persecution or Communist takeovers as refugees needing special consideration from the United States. This led to the Displaced Person Acts of 1948 and 1950, and the Refugee Relief Act of 1953 (see entry for 1953). Over 500,000 people were admitted to the United States under these acts regardless of existing restrictions in national immigration law. Immigration climbed to 0.9 million in the decade of 1940–49 (mostly after the war), and then to 2.5 million in 1950–59.

1946— Another change in the nation's approach to immigrants caused partly by World War II was the Luce-Cellar bill that granted citizenship to immigrants from the country of India that were already in the United States. They had previously been barred from citizenship because of their color. Dalip Singh Saund, an earlier Indian immigrant who had gained a Ph.D. from the University of California at Berkeley, worked tirelessly for the bill and eventually was elected to the House of Representatives in 1957 as the first Asian to hold a Congressional office.

The act also permitted Philippine-Americans already in the United States to seek to go through the naturalization process as well.

October 1, 1949— The communist forces of Mao Zedong, having driven the forces of Chiang Kai-Shek from mainland China to Taiwan, proclaimed the People's Republic of China and established a communist dictatorship in China. Ironically, China had emerged from a target of official immigration discrimination starting in 1882 to an ally of the United States in 1943 with re-established immigration rights. Immigration normalization lasted only six years.

Chinese refugees fleeing from Mao's government were generally welcomed in the West, but it was not initially easy to escape from China, and the United States was a very distant destination. Eventually the two countries would achieve a normal relationship of sorts, and by 2007 China would be recognized as an economic world power functioning along distinctly capitalistic lines within the communist dictatorship. Immigration relationships would also evolve to some degree of normality, and the once obscure nation of Taiwan would become an important economic player and a prime source of immigration to the United States.

June 27, 1952— The Immigration and Nationality Act (INA) of 1952 (often called the McCarran-Walter Act after its Congressional authors, Senator Pat McCarran of Nevada and Congressman Francis Walter of Pennsylvania) was passed by Congress after overriding a veto by President Truman. The bill is often mentioned as another piece of restrictive immigration legislation due to the politics of its authors. However, viewed objectively, this act contained benefits for many immigrants. One of its most notable aspects was that it basically removed the last racial and ethnic barriers to naturalization, even if it did continue the quota system of immigration. Further, an immigration preference system evolved favoring certain ethnic groups and placing great stress on labor qualifications.

The act did consolidate and continue much of the restrictive laws of the first part of the 20th century, but there were some important changes. The Asiatic Barred Act of 1917 (see entry for February 5, 1917) which had completely barred Asian immigrants from some areas was abolished. Further, immigrants from literally all nations of the world were now eligible for admission to the United States. The initial minimum quota was set at 100 persons annually. This was very low in many cases, but at least there were finally no exclusions in the immigration law based on national origin. This concept would continue to expand in future legislation. Some countries would block immigration based on their own internal laws, but the United States would no longer impose restrictions based on issues concerned with national origin.

The INA defined three classes of immigrants. The first was citizens of the United States who were exempt from quotas and who were to be admitted without restrictions. The second class was all other immigrants (except refugees) who were limited to a total of 270,000 admissions per year. The third class was refugees who met requirements specifically defined to help them. Nearly all of the debate concerning the act focused on the increased powers given the government to deport legal immigrants suspected of Communist sympathies and to similarly deny visas to anyone foreign person suspected of such sympathies. The act was a product of its time and the Cold War. There were other issues involved with the definition and implementation of its revised quota system, but actions involved with the anti–Communism part of the act grabbed most of the headlines.

It must be remembered that in 1952 eastern Europe was consolidated under the influence and control of the communist Soviet Union, mainland China had been taken over by a communist regime, and the Korean war was underway between the communist regime in North Korea (an ally of communist China) and the regime in South Korea (supported by the United States). Both Russia and China, our allies in World War II, were now (as noted before) our prime enemies. It is easy to understand that our basic immigration policies were sharply colored by anti-communistic feeling in Congress. For those immigrants specifically fleeing from communistic regimes, unusual benefits and help were available. These immigrants/refugees represented "victories" for the United States in the Cold War.

The McCarran-Walter bill expanded the existing quota system to all countries except those in the Western Hemisphere. It also introduced the first system of visa preferences in terms of giving preference to immigrants with certain skills and for the relatives of persons already within the United States. These preferences continued in future immigration laws up to today. But the new immigration law of 1965 (see entry for October 2, 1965) dismantled all of the national origin quotas with their flavor of racism.

July 25, 1952—Puerto Rico was proclaimed a commonwealth after a successful referendum held on May 3. Commonwealth status conferred more autonomy on the Puerto Rican government, but it did not change the fact that Puerto Ricans were, and had been since the Jones-Shafroth Act of 1917 (see entry for March 2, 1917), citizens of the United States.

In the battle over illegal immigrants at the end of the century and into the 21st century, this fact often seemed to be overlooked, especially in the northeast centered on New York City where many Puerto Ricans reside, although not necessarily fulltime. Their comings and goings between the northeast and Puerto Rico are simply a movement of citizens from one place to another, not a season movement such as illegal immigrants often make. Often the difference is not understood, and Puerto Ricans are subject to restrictions local residents wish to place on illegal immigrants.

1953— The Refugee Relief Act (PL 83–203) of 1953 was another recognition that World War II had created yet another class of immigrants needing special help on a humanitarian basis, and this act was meant to help refugees fleeing from the destruction of their home country (or its conversion to a dictatorship) as a result of the war. The problem had been noted just after the war in 1945 (see entry for September 2, 1945), but its extent and the number of refugees surpassed everyone's expectations. This specific act was focused on admitting 214,000 immigrants who had lived in the now communist countries of eastern Europe.

Refugee relief would be required almost indefinitely in the future as new wars and new dictatorships would produce an almost endless stream of refugees around the world, by whatever name they would be classified under. The issue of proper handling of those who are claiming refugee status and those claiming "asylum" has persisted until today (2007) and has no end in sight. It is an incredibly complex problem, the intermixing of the immigration laws of various countries (including the United States) and complicated protocols from such bodies as the United Nations (which as a member the United States is committed to follow). It would take another book this size to attempt to discuss the rules applying to asylum seekers and refugees escaping some catastrophe or another, and it is a subject far beyond the scope of this book. Suffice it to say that the mix of desperate persons, aggressive lawyers, and generally sympathetic courts results in an ever-growing number of persons seeking relief via admission to the United States, even if they often change the category of the class they are seeking relief under in response to what they see s an unfavorable ruling of some sort or another.

March 1, 1954— Five members of Congress were wounded in the House of Representatives by four Puerto Rican independence supporters who fired at random from the spectators' gallery. This followed an assassination attempt on President Truman in November of 1950 by two members of the Puerto Rico nationalist movement.

In spite of becoming a Commonwealth in 1952 (see entry for July 25, 1952) after a positive vote in a referendum May of 1952, there were still Puerto Rican fanatics who wanted to win with violence what they could not win at the ballot box, an all too familiar occurrence in the history of the world. Unfortunately, this argument over status within Puerto Rico would still be going on in the twenty-first century (see entry for April 25, 2007), although those desiring independence would have dwindled to a tiny minority by then. The 2007 argument would be about full-fledged statehood versus the existing Commonwealth status. Within Puerto Rico, the argument about its status vis-à-vis the United States had been going on almost constantly since the United States had acquired Puerto Rico after the Spanish-American war of 1898 (see entry for April 24, 1898).

1959— In a book published in 1959, noted Professor of History at Harvard University, Oscar Handlin, wrote of what he called the "end of immigration" in the United States in 1924 following the restrictive laws of that year (see entry for May 26, 1924). Handlin had previously won a Pulitzer Prize for his 1951 book about immigration titled *The Uprooted*, a compassionate historical look at immigration in the United States that had much of the flavor of a novel.

In his 1959 book, *Immigration as a Factor in American History*, Handlin wrote a more conventional narrative history of immigration, but in his conclusion to the book he bemoaned the fact that as late as more than a decade after World War II, he saw no sign of a reversal of the restrictive immigration act of 1924. Handlin acknowledged the "temporary" measures "to offer asylum to some refugees of war-torn Europe," but he focused on the 1952 McCarran-Walter Act (see entry for June 27, 1952), which he saw as a continuation of the restrictive 1924 act, and he concluded that there was no reason to be optimistic about positive immigration changes in the near future.

Forecasting the future in any field is fraught with danger, but it is surprising that such an experienced student in the field as Professor Handlin could miss the stirrings in the nation and in Congress that would lead to perhaps the single most dramatic change in immigration laws in 1965, a change that would become the most significant in immigration at the time in the nation's history. Immigration historians speak almost nostalgically of the about 38 million immigrants that arrived in the United States in the first 150 years of its existence. But in the 60 years after 1950, a similar number would arrive through the first decade of the 21st century, and if illegal immigrants were counted, the total would approach 50 million.

The age of the highest immigration in the history of the United States is right now, not some distant date in the past. And the time of cumulatively the least restrictive immigration laws in history took place just before the new century. In that context, the debates of 2005 through 2007 are the most important in the history of immigration legislation as the country realized that illegal immigration was the issue that needed restrictive legislation while legal immigration could continue in its liberalized status quo. As often happens, the present time going on around us is the prime decision time in immigration legislation, not some distant time in the past.

January 1959— Fidel Castro took over as the leader of Cuba, and after some initial misleading statements that he was not a communist, installed a communist regime in Cuba of which he was the dictator. He aligned himself with the Soviet Union, and became a follower of its policies. The United States was greatly displeased to have a communist regime only 90 miles from its coastline and the Soviet Union was greatly pleased. But after the abortive Bay of Pigs invasion in 1961, when the United States supported Cuban dissidents who were crushed, and the Cuban missile crisis in 1962, when Russia backed down and withdrew the missiles it had brought into Cuba, an uneasy peace was maintained between Cuba and the United States, while the United States imposed various economic embargoes on Cuba

Immigration from Cuba became a notable issue because of Cuba's high visibility in the Cold War. Cuban refugees were highly encouraged to come to the United States, where they received unusually good treatment as examples of the shortcomings of communism in the eyes of the United States. As noted in this chronology, there was essentially a constant flow of Cubans fleeing to the nearby United States in various types of small boats in the next four decades, and two massive boat lifts in 1965 and 1980 (see entries for September 28, 1965 and March 28, 1980) that were triggered by actions of Fidel Castro and counter-responses by the United States. In "normal" years, 30,000 Cubans annually would reach the United States before declining closer to 20,000 near the end of the century. A large and rather prosperous Cuban-American community would develop in the Miami area.

December 31, 1959— The end of the last year of the 1950s marked the peak of the "bracero" program. This program essentially permitted agricultural workers (mostly from Mexico) to enter the United States to work in the "factories in the field" of large (and small) agricultural companies. The program was especially popular in California, and the agricultural interests there grew readily "addicted" to such (cheap) workers, an addiction that would have a substantial impact on future problems with illegal immigration.

Between 1955 and 1959, more than 400,000 such workers were admitted in every year, while at least 200,000 were admitted in each year between 1951 and 1964. The bracero program is connected with World War II in the minds of many people because the program was tried as a wartime experiment in the 1940s when so many soldiers were off to war. But in the 1940s the program involved an average of only 50,000 workers (no year reached a peak of 100,000), while the numbers after 1950 were much higher as noted above.

The bracero program officially ended on December 31, 1964, after continuing strong opposition by groups interested in labor and welfare overcame agriculture business interests in Congress. But there was no overcoming reality, as is the case so often with immigration bills. The peak of 400,000 workers per year at the end of the 1950s showed both the needs of the agricultural business and the number of workers available and anxious to fill those needs. The missing bracero workers readily became illegal immigrants from Mexico, thus launching the single biggest immigration issue since the liberalization of immigration in 1965 (see entry for October 2, 1965) and today.

December 26, 1960— An airlift ultimately called Operation Peter Pan (Operacion Pedro Pan) began between Cuba and the United States, and went on for nearly two years until October 23, 1962 (when it stopped due to the Cuban Missile Crisis). In total about 14,000 children were brought to the United States from Cuba. The stated purpose of the operation was to transport children of parents who opposed the new Communist regime in Cuba, and later the operation included children of parents frightened by rumors that their children would be shipped to work camps in Russia or eastern Europe. The children were sent to the United States alone as teenagers or in small groups including toddlers, and for a while the operation was clandestine. Catholic groups, coordinated by Father Bryan Walsh of the United States, gave a great deal of assistance to the operation.

The name of the operation came from jargon in which Miami and the United States was dubbed "Never-Never Land" and the commercial operator of the flights used was Pan-Am Airways. The original intention of the operation was that their parents would join the children in a matter of months. However, the Bay of Pigs invasion by the United States in 1961 and the subsequent missile crisis in 1962 ultimately caused the operation to turn to other means to care for the children when it became clear that many of the parents would be unable to leave Cuba even via other countries to come to the United States.

The operation became controversial in retrospect as the Central Intelligence Agency (CIA) of the United States was accused of employing it as just another way to sow discord in the new Communist regime and aid in its downfall. However, one group or another has accused the CIA of nearly every evil on earth, and objective evidence of its involvement is hard to obtain. Operation Peter Pan was neither the first nor the last such operation involving the movement of children between nations in or after a time of war.

1962 — The Migration and Refugee Assistance Act was passed to deal with "unexpected and urgent needs" of refugees, displaced persons, conflict victims, and similar persons at risk around the world. The ongoing nature of the problem is demonstrated by the fact the act was used nearly 40 years later to deal with problems in the Balkans and Nepal.

September 28, 1965 — Fidel Castro announced that any Cuban with relatives in the United States who wanted to leave Cuba could do so after October 10. President Johnson of the United States used the signing of the momentous 1965 immigration bill four days later (see next entry) as an opportunity to respond to Castro's offer. Johnson proclaimed that Cubans who seek refuge in the United States would find it.

The process began in October at a small port east of Havana called Camarioca. Small vessels, both from Cuba and those sent from South Florida relatives of those in Cuba, began the exodus, with the United

States Coast Guard doing its best to assist the many small boats not really seaworthy. By November 10, 1965, the United States and Cuba signed a Memorandum of Understanding that would give each side some control over who could leave and who would be expected at the other end. This was a far cry from the chaotic Mariel Boat Lift that would take place in 1980 (see entry for March 28, 1980).

In what was dubbed "Operation Sealift," three good-sized ships were sent to Camarioca during mid–November and brought back a total of about 4,600 refugees. Castro then closed the port and arrangements were made to begin regular flights by two chartered aircraft a day between the United States and Varadero, a small airport outside Havana. The flights ran regularly until August of 1971, and then less regularly as the Cuban government began to interfere. The last flight took place in April of 1973, ending an airlift that saw about 3,000 flights bringing almost 300,000 Cuban refugees to the United States over a seven-year period. But even without an organized effort, about 185,000 more Cuban refugees made it to the United States before the Muriel boatlift in 1980 (an average exceeding 30,000 annually, which was 50 percent higher than the supposed maximum of 20,000 for any one country per existing immigration laws of the time).

The majority of these Cubans settled in the Miami area, forming what was called "Little Havana," where no English was necessary or even useful in some areas. The U.S. government gave the Cuban refugees excellent benefits to the point where complaints were made than the Cuban immigrants got better benefits than poor American citizens. But the unspoken point was that the Cuban refugees were a sort of trophy for the United States in the Cold War with Russia, representing people who made a conscious choice to leave the Communistic regime in Cuba in favor of the United States. The Cuban refugees, especially early on, were an elite mix of businessmen and managers, and Little Havana became a prosperous area for people establishing and running businesses of all types.

The Cuban refugees were also politically inclined, and as more refugees continually arrived and more gained citizenship, they became a potent voting bloc in south Florida. Eventually Cuban-Americans would occupy local positions up to Mayor of Miami, and would represent Florida in the House of Representatives and the Senate. Following the Elian Gonzalez case in 1999–2000 (see entry for November 25, 1999), Cuban-Americans played a big part in denying Al Gore the electoral votes of Florida (and hence the Presidency) in the 2000 presidential election.

October 2, 1965— Using the Statue of Liberty as a backdrop, President Lyndon Johnson signed by far the most sweeping changes in liberalizing immigration law in the nation's history prior to the 21st century. The changes were made by amendments to the Immigration and Nationality Act of 1965. The act was also known as the Hart-Celler Act. It was proposed by Emmanuel Celler and strongly supported by Ted Kennedy.

The 1965 Act abolished the quotas that had been in place since 1924 (see entry for May 26, 1924). In 1965 immigration limits were expanded to 170,000 persons annually for all nations in the Eastern Hemisphere, with a limit of 20,000 to any one nation. The total was set at 120,000 annually in the Western Hemisphere (by 1968). Further, to make up for past discrimination, preferences for nations in the Eastern Hemisphere were given to close relatives of American citizens, refugees, and persons with certain job skills. Persons in Western Hemisphere nations were eligible for visas only on a first-come first-served basis, but spouses, children, and parents of American citizens were exempt from numerical limitations as well as special classes of immigrants.

The 1965 version of the immigration laws was essentially an extension of the Civil Rights revolution that was taking place in the United States in the 1960s. Lyndon Johnson had been elected president in a landslide in 1964 following the assassination of President Kennedy in 1963, and Johnson had substantial margins in both houses of Congress. Johnson could pass any Civil Rights legislation he wanted to, and he did exactly that. Johnson decided not to run for president in 1968 because of the unpopularity of the war in Vietnam, and many of his Civil Rights initiatives were overturned or watered down in the years that followed. However, the dramatic changes in immigration law remained the same or were even more liberalized as time went on.

Nothing was the same in immigration law after 1965, and that year still stands as a great landmark in immigration law in changes of both the concept and implementation of immigration laws. Practically all the issues in immigration today, except perhaps the startling rise of illegal immigration, can be traced back to the changes made in 1965. If the time prior to the 1880s is considered a time of little restriction on (or even attention to) immigration, and the next 75 years is considered a time of specific restrictions on immigration, the time after 1965 can be considered a time of inviting the world to become legal immigrants, and that time is still going on today for legal immigrants.

The number of immigrants entering the United States grew steadily after the immigration laws of 1965 were passed. Over four million came in the 1970s, over six million in the 1980s, and over 9 million in the 1990s (the total in the first decade of the 21st century will probably approach 10 million even excluding the presence of an estimated 12 million illegal immigrants). The official number of over 9 million in the 1990s is still the largest ever for a decade, but it actually included a substantial number of previously illegal immigrants who had been in the United States for some time and were granted amnesty. They were officially counted as "new" immigrants.

The problem of illegal immigrants became a big one in the decades after 1965, and has remained so to this date. As is noted in the rest of this chronology, attempts to solve the problem failed because of an inability by Congress to reach agreement on root causes and solutions, and a generous dose of naiveté. Many people have strong emotional reactions to the problem of illegal immigration, and attempts to reach a "middle ground" between those strongly supporting the illegal immigrants and those strongly opposed may have failed simply because there is no middle ground in this debate.

It is clear that the 1965 laws (and their full efficacy in 1968) caused a substantial change in the national origins of immigrants. Reflecting the fact that many Congresses in the United States do not clearly understand the full implications of the laws they pass regarding immigration, the 1965 law was widely expected to cause a new surge in European immigration. However, over 80 percent of the new immigrants in the decades following the 1965 revisions came from Latin America, the Caribbean, or Asia. The leading countries since 1970 are Mexico (accounting for 20 percent of all immigrants), the Philippines, China, India, South Korea, Vietnam, and the Dominican Republic. Part of this is due to the large population increases in South America and Asia compared to an actual decline in much of Europe, but the most significant factor is still the change in immigration laws since 1965.

1975

To some extent the biggest change caused by the 1965 law, even if often unnoticed by Congress, was that the sources of immigration changed dramatically. As noted, by the 1980s, more than 80 percent of all legal immigrants came from Asia and Latin America. If illegal immigrants were added, the percentage from these areas would exceed 90 percent. The 1965 law to this extent turned immigration on its head compared to all prior years.

Spring 1975— President Gerald Ford authorized an operation, known as Operation Baby Lift, to airlift several thousand war orphans out of Vietnam for adoption in other countries including the United States. More than 2,700 children came to the United States, and about 1,300 more were flown to Canada, Europe, and Australia.

As with almost any humanitarian operation of its type, there were controversies after the fact because the operation was not absolutely perfect. There were questions as to whether all of the children involved were actually orphans, and whether being transported to other countries was in the best interest of all the children. An absolutely unanswerable question raised after the fact by those standing on the sidelines.

May 16, 1975— Congress approved spending of $405 million to assist refugees from South Vietnam. A total of about 140,000 refugees were eventually flown to the United States as a result of this action.

1978— An amendment to the Immigration and Nationality Act abolished separate quotas for each hemisphere and instead authorized a total annual quota worldwide of 290,000 immigrants to the United States, with a maximum 20,000 for any one country. Actually, these limits are almost meaningless because they apply only to immigrants applying under numerical restrictions. Those immigrants to which such numerical restrictions do not apply (of which there are many categories), greatly increase the actual numbers. For example, by 1985, listing only the three leading groups, 61,000 Mexicans were admitted, 48,000 Filipinos, and 35,000 Koreans. Once again, what the law said and the real world was quite different.

In addition, many potential immigrants chose to avoid what they considered unfavorable quotas for their countries by resorting to illegal immigration. Many immigrants from physically nearby countries such as Mexico, with a long history of "informally" crossing the border to work, had long been utilizing illegal immigration to avoid waiting (and paying) for legal entry.

Illegal immigration did not involve just trying to cross an unguarded section of the border around the United States. It was estimated that at least 40 percent of all illegal immigrants were made up of persons who legally obtained visas for a short visit to the United States (easily acquired) and then did not leave when the visa expired. There was no simple way to track such immigrants.

March 17, 1980—The Refugee Act of 1980 reduced the quota for total annual immigration to 270,000 from 290,000, excluding refugees. Demonstrating again its almost ludicrous lack of understanding about immigration issues, Congress believed the "normal flow" of refugees and asylum-seekers at 50,000 per year. However, since 1980, the United States has admitted an average of 85,000 refugees and 7,000 asylum-seekers annually. This is almost double the original estimate.

One problem with immigration estimates is a lack both of good data and good understanding of the data that does exist and its implications. But every immigration law in the late 1900s was full of exceptions and special considerations, and an often-fuzzy definition of exactly who qualifies as a "refugee" or an "asylum" seeker. Under the 1980 Act the president sets the annual maximum number of refugees, but the number can be adjusted upward during the year in response to a "humanitarian" crisis. The result is always a larger number of immigrants than originally expected, but many American citizens feel this result is just right. Ironically, only a month after the 1980 law was signed, the Mariel boatlift (see next entry) started in Cuba almost as a demonstration of the futility of trying to predict how many refugees would be reasonably admitted in the future via any immigration law.

March 28, 1980—This date essentially marked the beginning of the so-called Mariel boatlift between Cuba and the United States that ran for about six months between April and October in 1980. The immediate cause of the boatlift took place on March 28, 1980, when a Cuban national named Hector Sanyustiz smashed a bus through a fence of the Peruvian embassy in Havana. Sanyustiz asked for asylum for himself and four others on the bus. The original driver of the bus, who had declared a non-existent breakdown of the bus so that all the regular riders would disembark, was on the bus with three other plotters when it crashed through the embassy fence.

Unfortunately, a Cuban guard was killed in the crossfire that took place when several guards fired at the bus in an attempt to prevent it from smashing into the embassy fence. Although the Peruvian Ambassador granted the request for asylum for the men on the bus, Fidel Castro insisted the five men be returned to stand trial for the death of the guard. Peru refused, and Castro then threatened to remove all guards protecting the embassy. He did so on Good Friday, April 4.

News of the action spread throughout Havana via word-of-mouth, and by Easter Sunday (April 6), more than 10,000 people had crammed into the grounds of the Peruvian Embassy seeking asylum. The overcrowding was severe enough to be dangerous. The United States agreed to take 3,500 people, and nine other nations agreed to take about 7,500 more. An airlift to Costa Rica got underway to process more, but Castro then canceled the flights in a dispute with the United States. Finally, caught on the wrong end of what was becoming a negative story about Cuba around the world, Castro next proclaimed that anyone who wanted to leave Cuba could do so as long as someone would come to the small port town of Mariel and pick them up. He invited Cuban exiles in the United States to come retrieve their relatives in Cuba.

This proclamation set off a "Freedom Flotilla" from south Florida to Cuba that began on April 21, 1980. The Mariel boatlift had begun. By the time it ended on October 1, 1980, about 125,000 Cubans had emigrated to the nearby United States. There was chaos along the way at almost every step in the process. At Mariel, the over 1,700 boats that arrived during the boatlift were sometimes packed to the gills with all comers from Cuba regardless of who the boats had come to rescue. This was much different than the boatlift and subsequent airlift that started in September of 1965 (see entry for September 28, 1965) which was tightly controlled on both sides every step of the way.

Stories later surfaced that Castro had freed prisoners from jail as well as patients from mental health hospitals and cynically sent them to Mariel to be packed unto boats waiting at the docks. One overloaded boat overturned at sea and 14 migrants died. It later turned out that only 2,746 persons of the about 125,000 Cubans involved in the boatlift (about two percent) were violent criminals by the standards of the United States and were denied asylum. It must be remembered that simply criticizing the government was a "crime" punishable by being sent to jail in Communist Cuba.

In Miami chaos also reigned in the immigration processing centers as the Cubans from the boatlift poured ashore. The government was forced to open additional processing centers around the country, including one in Fort Chafee, Arkansas, where crowded conditions quickly became unmanageable. In the category of unintended consequences, the defeat of then Governor Bill Clinton in his re-election bid in 1980 was blamed by many on the poor handling of the events at Fort Chafee. President Jimmy Carter also received heavy criticism for his handling of the Mariel boatlift. But Carter's massive defeat in the 1980 elections by Ronald Reagan was so overwhelming and there were so many problems with the Carter administration that analysts felt his mishandling of the Mariel event was not a decisive issue.

Castro finally closed the port of Mariel on September 26, 1980, and ordered all boats awaiting passengers to leave. Accordingly, a tent city that had been built in Miami to help in the processing of the Cuban migrants was taken down on September 30, 1980. Except for recriminations and some after-the-fact legislation to clarify the status of and assistance due to the people who came on the exodus from Cuba, the Mariel boatlift was over. It was an excellent example how the careful analysis that went into an Immigration Act such as that passed only 11 days before the Mariel boatlift started (see entry for March 28, 1980) can be overtaken by events as soon as only a matter of days.

July 1980—An incident involving a 13-year-old Russian boy named Walter Polovchak demonstrated how far the Immigration Laws could be twisted "in the national interest" when something as emotional as scoring points in the Cold War was involved. A Russian couple had come to the United States on immigrant visas, bringing their 13-year-old son, an older daughter (Natalie) and a younger daughter to Chicago. After being in the United States for five months, the couple decided to return to Russia. However, 13-year-old Walter and his older sister Natalie did not want to return to Russia. They ran away to the home of a cousin, an established Chicago resident.

The police took the teenagers into custody after being called by the parents. However, after hearing of the case, the Immigration and Naturalization Service (INS) and the State Department advised the police not to return the children to the custody of their parents as was the normal procedure. The government then arranged for the children to file for asylum under the new 1980 immigration law (see entry for March 17, 1980). The parents hired a lawyer, filed suit for the custody of Walter (but not his older sister Natalie), and left to return to Russia with their younger daughter as planned.

An Illinois court quickly ruled for the parents, but the State Department claimed it was "not in the national interest" for Walter to go home, ultimately throwing the case into Federal Court. The State Department was well aware of how slowly the Federal Courts moved, and they stalled as much as possible, hoping to delay a decision for as long as five years until October 3, 1985, when Walter would be 18 years old and could make his own decision legally according to the law in both the United States and Russia.

The plan almost worked, but the case finally came to trial on July 17, 1985, a little less than five years later. A federal district court found for the parents. The government filed an appeal, and the Seventh Circuit Court heard the case on September 9, 1985. It only took one day for the court to rule that the government had clearly violated the rights of the parents. However, with only weeks to go before Walter reached maturity, the Court stayed any action until the day came on October 3. Walter Polovchak then happily expressed his desire to continue to stay in the United States. The parents had clearly been denied justice, but the Cold Was the Cold War. Once again, justice delayed was justice denied.

Some members of the Cuban Community in Miami hoped to use the Polovchak case as a precedent two decades later in the celebrated case of Elian Gonzalez (see entry for November 25, 1999), but not only were the facts different but the Cold War was over and Russia had imploded a decade before. There was no organized government effort to intervene to keep Elian Gonzalez in the United States; there was rather an effort to return him to Cuba. A different sense of justice for different times.

1981— A commission led by Father Theodore M. Hesburgh, the ex-president of Notre Dame University, which was called the Select Commission on Immigration and Refugee Policy (SCIRP) made its report to Congress (the commission had been created by Congress in 1978). The report stated that illegal immigration was the top immigration problem in the country, and it recommended cutting back on immigration in total. However, the report recommended following the basic changes of the landmark 1965 law (see entry for October 2, 1965), and it further proposed an amnesty for the illegal immigrants already here while tightening border controls.

Hesburgh personally was ahead of his time in proposing an updated Social Security card for everyone, with microchip carrying essential information as a means of addressing illegal immigration, but his colleagues on the commission would not go along with his views. The SCIRP report became the basis of the 1986 immigration bill declaring amnesty (see entry for November 6, 1986), but the suggestions for better border control were not intelligently followed.

June 15, 1982— The Supreme Court issued a ruling that a Texas law permitting the withholding of state funds for the education of illegal immigrants was unconstitutional because it violated the equal protection clause of the Fourteenth Amendment. This was another unintended consequence of the 14th Amendment (see entry for July 28, 1868) that would place an untenable financial burden on states with large numbers on illegal immigrants, especially as the number of illegal immigrants in the United States reached an estimated 12 million in 2007.

The Court ruled that although illegal immigrants are not citizens, they are "people" and thus are afforded 14th Amendment protections. Their children would be severely disadvantaged by the lack of an education, and since Texas could not show that its regulation served a "compelling state interest," the Texas law was struck down.

At the time there were "only" about three or four million illegal immigrants in the United States, and many people agreed that having a block of their children essentially wandering around during school hours was not desirable. However, as the number of illegal immigrants continued to grow, and the costs of providing free services to them as mandated by the courts also continued to grow, resentment built and finally resulted in Proposition 187 in California in 1994 (see entry for November 1994). The resentment continued to grow after Proposition 187 was struck down by the courts, and it was this resentment that came to full flower in the battle over the immigration bill of 2007.

November 6, 1986— The Immigration Reform and Control Act of 1986 (also known as the Simpson-Mazzoli bill or IRCA) was an attempt by Congress, in its often bumbling way when it came to immigration, to reduce illegal immigration. The Act granted amnesty to those illegal immigrants who had lived continuously in the United States since January 1, 1982, and to others who were working in agriculture. About 2.8 million illegal immigrants eventually obtained legal status through this amnesty, and the total is much higher if all the family members later brought into the country through its extensions and expansions are included.

Critics claimed that the amnesty gave birth to a blizzard of counterfeit documents, which were claimed to show that many illegal immigrants qualified for the amnesty. The critics added that so-called "undocumented" aliens simply became aliens with counterfeit documents. Further, in yet another ludicrous statement about immigration, Congress took the position that the new law would end illegal immigration afterwards because it mandated penalties for employers who knowingly hired illegal immigrants.

With employers (including many private citizens) anxious to benefit from the low wages paid to illegal immigrants, this part of the law was basically ignored. Many communities forbade the police to ask about the legal status of immigrants involved in a criminal act so as to insure cooperation with the law when investigations were made about illegal activities. Some communities who felt sympathy for illegal immigrants forbade cooperation of any sort with the immigration laws that might result in an eventual deportation. The clear strategy for any illegal immigrant was to hunker down and wait for the next amnesty. Additional illegal immigrants poured into the United States planning to enjoy its benefits while employing the same strategy.

Some critics have estimated that for every illegal immigrant granted amnesty under this plan, approximately four new illegal immigrants replaced them by 2007. This brought the estimated number of illegal immigrants to about 12 million by 2007. Further, the number of immigrants who benefited from the amnesty is far more than the "official" number of 2.8 million because of the number of relatives subsequently brought into the United States by those granted amnesty. Thus, these critics point out that granting amnesty is a poor way of dealing with the illegal immigration problem because it simply encourages more illegal immigration, and there is no good way to determine how many immigrants will enter the United States as a result of any new amnesty.

The almost complete failure of the 1986 legislation to reduce subsequent illegal immigration would become a major factor in the debate over legislation in 2007 to complete another immigration bill with amnesty (see entries for June 3, 7, 14, and 28, 2007). The 1986 results would be quoted as evidence that the federal government does not have the will to control illegal immigration no matter what rhetoric it employs.

November 29, 1990— The Immigration Act of 1990 established an annual ceiling of 700,000 immigrants for each of the following three years, and a ceiling of 675,000 annually thereafter. These numbers excluded refugees. Amnesty was extended to the family members of those illegal immigrants who had taken advantage of the amnesty of 1986 (see entry for November 6, 1986) and who had taken steps to become citizens of the United States.

While family members of citizens of the United States remained the largest single category of legal immigrants, the 1990 act established a separate annual quota of 140,000 for immigrants who had special job skills. In addition, the 1990 Act granted special annual quotas ranging from 40,000 to 55,000 to countries from which few immigrants had come in recent years. Also, individuals who had invested over $1 million dollars in business ventures in the United States that created jobs for citizens of the United States received preferential treatment. Further, the 1990 Act gave special consideration to political refugees who were escaping from countries with repressive governments.

Critics of the 1990 law stated that as far as immigration laws were concerned, words such as "special" and "preferential" had lost their meaning.

1990

There was almost no end of categories defined as "special" intended for use by various lobbying organizations that espoused a "special" group requiring "preferential" treatment. In the eyes of these critics the immigration doors had been swung wide open for all comers as long as Congress could invent a "special" group to whom preference should be given. But these critics found little support because the mood in the country, to the extent any attention was paid to immigration laws, was the more the merrier.

Perhaps the part of the 1990 law with the strongest implication for the future was what was called temporary protected status (TPS). In addition to the many categories of "special" circumstances for legal immigrants, TPS was a special category for even illegal immigrants. If illegal immigrants apprehended in the United States could claim they would suffer hardship if they were deported to their country of origin because of an ongoing armed conflict, environmental disaster, or other extraordinary condition, the INS was given the power by the 1990 law to grant yet another "special" exception to allow the illegal immigrants to live and work in the United States until conditions improved in their homeland.

The Attorney General of the United States was given the power to designate countries qualifying for TPS, and the concept was that once the "special" circumstance resulting in the TPS was over, the illegal immigrants would then be ultimately deported. Countries designated for TPS status have included Guatemala, El Salvador, Angola, Burundi, Liberia, Sierra Leone, Somalia, and Sudan.

Critics of TPS have pointed out that the definition of who qualifies is strictly in the eye of the beholder, and that there is nothing more permanent than a "temporary" government program. The net effect of the TPS program has been to substantially increase the number of illegal immigrants flooding into the United States both as a vehicle for doing so and as an example encouraging others to come on the basis that someday there will be a "special" exception made for them as well. The critics further noted that it was hard to tell if members of Congress, when it came to immigration, were especially benevolent, or hopelessly naïve, or had some hidden agenda in mind. Considering that the number of illegal immigrants in the United States has grown to an estimated 12 million in 2007 from an estimated three million after the amnesty of 1986, the answer would seem to be a mix of all three factors.

1992— The Chinese Student Protection Act was yet another ad hoc immigration law giving "special" protection to Chinese students who were caught between being in the United States as students and the political turmoil taking place in China in the aftermath of the Tiananmen Square protests of 1989.

May 14, 1993— A plebiscite in Puerto Rico supported continuing its commonwealth status with the United States. It was another in the seemingly endless actions taken to clarify the status between Puerto Rico and the United States since Puerto Rico was ceded to the United States after the Spanish-American War of 1898 (see entry for April 24, 1898). The issue would still be festering in Puerto Rico in 2007 (see entry for April 25, 2007).

August 15, 1994— President Clinton reversed more than three decades of immigration policy by announcing that Cuban boat people or rafters (called *balseros* in Cuba) who were picked up at sea by the Coast Guard would no longer be taken to Miami to be paroled into the United States to receive the normal benefits given to refugees from Cuba. Those picked up would be taken to the United States naval base at Guantanamo, Cuba, and not paroled into the United States. The only options available at Guantanamo would be to return to Cuba or be sent to a third country. Guantanamo was selected because the long arm of the federal courts in the United States did not reach there and this eliminated the possibility that a sympathetic federal judge would intervene in a deportation hearing.

Clinton's pronouncement was prompted by the fact that although balseros had been reaching the United States for some time, poorer economic circumstances in Cuba caused by the fall of the Soviet Union, and an increased number of balseros, often putting to sea in non-seaworthy boats assuming they would receive Coast Guard help, began to strain relations with Castro, who desperately wanted a relaxation of the ongoing economic embargo by the United States. Castro finally publicly threatened in mid–August to permit another mass emigration to the United States along the lines of the Mariel boatlift in 1980 (see entry for March 28, 1980).

The Clinton administration replied that it would not permit such a boatlift and promised a naval blockade of Cuba if such a boatlift were attempted. The Miami Cuban community cooperated by advising its members not to send boats to Cuba to pick up relatives if Castro took any action towards a boatlift. Actually, about 15,000 Cubans yearly were being admitted to the United States in the 1980s and 1990s, most during a time when the two countries agreed to immigration of about 20,000 per year, primarily for family reunification. In addition, balseros continued to reach the mainland of the United States on their own and received the normally generous welcome from the United States. As noted, Castro was pursuing some easing of the economic embargo, which Clinton could not consider in any manner in an election year.

November 1994— The fall elections in California produced an over-whelming victory for Proposition 187 (nearly 60 percent of the voters favored it), which Pete Wilson rode to a reelection win in the race for Governor. Proposition 187 appeared to be unconstitutional on its face as it proposed to deny a number of state benefits to illegal immigrants, including free schooling. Aside from running afoul of the law permitting only the federal government to legislate matters of immigration, the issue of charging illegal immigrants for the costs of their education had been rejected by the Supreme Court on the grounds of equal protection under the law in a Texas case in 1982.

Proposition 187 was in fact rejected by the courts, but observers noted that it drew a new line of active actions against illegal immigrants in a number of states across the nation. This action festered for over a decade, and by the end of 2005 helped in the creation of a House bill that was anti-illegal immigrant to the extent that it proposed to make illegal immigration a felony, and also proposed to criminalize those providing assistance to illegal immigrants (see entry for December 16, 2005). The House bill did not become law, but the attitude behind it would result in protracted debate on the landmark 2007 immigration bill in which many Senators reflected their constituents' desire for more aggressive enforcement of the immigration law and some special funding to insure it was carried out. Even President Bush noted that people no longer believed the federal government would do what it promised in terms of enforcing anti-illegal immigrant provisions in the proposed 2007 law.

Proposition 187 was credited by some groups with giving voice to a growing resentment in the United States to the "catch 22" aspect of immigration law that only the federal government could regulate immigration, but the federal government was unable or unwilling to stop illegal immigration. It then handed the bill to the states via other government laws for providing free schooling, free healthcare via emergency rooms, and various welfare benefits (either illegally or to citizen children of illegal immigrants born here) to the illegal immigrants the government essentially invited into the country. Even though rejected by the courts as noted, Proposition 187 turned out to have deep roots and affected local anti-illegal measures that became common in the United States during 2006 and after (see entries for March 25 and May 1, 2006).

1996 — Before the 1996 Presidential Election, partly due to the lingering influence of 1994's Proposition 187 (see entry for November 1994), adjustments to immigration law were made in April, August, and September of 1996 to tighten what had become an incredibly loose set of immigration laws, but the changes had only mixed results. The Illegal Immigration and Immigrant Responsibility Act (IIIRA) made it easier to deport illegal immigrants, and it established an income test for those attempting to bring family members into the United States where they often moved immediately onto the welfare rolls. Further, illegal immigrants who remained in the United States for more than six months were barred from re-entering for three years and those who remained in the United States for more than a year were barred from re-entering for ten years.

The 1996 Acts also expanded the list of crimes for which even legal immigrants can be deported, and attempted to restrict the right of immigrants to appeal INS rulings to federal courts. Reflecting the very ambiguous feelings many American citizens had towards immigration, federal judges generally are very receptive to claims, no matter how apparently specious, of discrimination or unequal treatment under the law. Deportation hearings quickly clog the courts for further review, and in many cases immigrants and their lawyers avidly pursue delay and hope for immigration law changes in their favor.

One of the 1996 laws had the unwieldy title on the Anti-Terrorism and Effective Death Penalty Act. It eliminated all INS discretion relative to deportation hearings for individuals who have criminal convictions.

Congress wanted to deport such individuals more or less automatically without the interference of the generally much more liberal courts. But in 1999 the Supreme Court ruled that the law could not be applied to deportation hearings that began prior to 1996. Once again the courts insisted on being involved in deportation hearings where they generally found some reason, nearly any reason in the view of critics, to prevent a deportation.

To some extent the courts often did not have to look too deeply to find a reason to prevent a deportation. The flood of immigration laws since 1965 were all generally favorable to immigration with many special exceptions for immigrants of all types (see 1990 for example), and all of these laws remained on the books more or less permanently. Even new laws seen as slightly more restrictive (such as this 1996 law, for example) did not rescind prior laws but simply added new issues or further relaxed old laws. The thicket of immigration law became ever denser, and a judge (or a "helpful" defense lawyer) could often raise issues that seemed contradictory or discriminatory and that would delay the deportation for further review. Few people in Congress at the time wanted to appear more restrictive on immigration by proposing the elimination of laws that appeared too favorable to immigrants.

1997 — As if in embarrassment for passing laws in 1996 (see previous entry) that could be possibly viewed as being generally more restrictive, Congress in 1997 passed legislation that would be more liberal, especially for illegal immigrants. This law, called the Nicaraguan Adjustment and Central American Relief Act, granted amnesty to Nicaraguans who had entered the United States illegally before December 1995. It also allowed certain Salvadorans and Guatemalans already in the country to suspend their deportation proceedings and apply for United States residency. Hundreds of thousands of Central Americans already in the country illegally who were not covered by the Act simply continued to seek residency by applying for asylum.

Even supporters of illegal immigrants criticized the Congress for applying Immigration law on essentially an ad hoc basis, responding to some complaints and not others. The Temporary Protected Status (TPS) law of 1990 (see entry for November 29, 1990) was nearly arbitrarily being applied to some civil wars that had been claimed to be going on for 20 years (hardly what could be called "temporary"), while not being applied to other seemingly similar situations. The lesson learned from this law, those opposed to illegal immigration claimed, was to come to the United States illegally, clamor for amnesty, and wait for the next law passed by Congress that would grant it in some form. In the meantime, the United States Census Bureau estimated that 8.7 million illegal immigrants lived in the United States in 2000 and the number was steadily growing. There was no sign the Congress knew how to deal with the problem.

1998 — New Laws— Two more immigration law changes that critics claimed were in the "excuse mode" of the 1997 laws (see entry for 1997) were passed in 1998. The first came in February when an insertion into the Agriculture Research Reform Act restored eligibility for Food Stamps to certain "qualified aliens." The second came in October with the passage of the Non-Citizen Benefit Clarification Act. This act created a new category of "nonqualified aliens" as a means of restoring Medicaid and SSI benefits removed in previous acts.

Illegal Immigrants were prime beneficiaries of both the 1997 and 1998 acts, and critics noted that since the expected development of "hard line" attitudes by the voters as a result of Proposition 187 in 1994 (see entry for November 1994) had not appeared to be a major factor in the elections, Congress went back to its "give everything to immigrants, illegal or not" attitudes. Other observers claimed the laws were only restoring "fairness" to all immigrants. The stage was continuing to be set for the unprecedented illegal immigration battles of the beginning of the 21st century.

1998 — Benefit Studies— The National Research Council published a study carried out by a group of distinguished economists from the National Academy of Sciences trying to answer the controversial question of whether immigrants produced a net gain to or a net drain on national resources. Both sides of the debate, as usual, cited selective facts to support their side of the issue. But this time two Harvard economists involved in the process felt the need to comment in an Op Ed article in the *New York Times* that stated that immigration had both positive and negative economic impacts, and that pro-immigration forces using the study to demonstrate only the good effects were failing to look at the whole picture. "Overall," they concluded, "the academy report is not a one-sided pro-immigration tract."

1998 — New York Statistics— In her book *From Ellis Island to JFK*, published in 2000, Nancy Foner points out that as of 1998 a new wave of immigration was taking place in New York City. The accompanying new wave of immigration in the United States was not occurring only in the southwestern states where most of the present attention on immigration has been focused in recent years.

In New York City, more than 2.5 million immigrants have arrived between the immigration reform of 1965 (see entry for October 2, 1965) and 1998. They were still arriving at the rate of over 100,000 per year in 1998. The foreign-born population of New York City in 1998 was 37.4 percent. This was the highest percentage recorded compared to prior census years since 1910, when the percentage was 40.8 percent. At that time, new immigration arrivals swarmed around Ellis Island, and in 1910, consisted primarily of eastern European Jews and southern Italians whose descendents still populate much of New York City. In 1998 the new wave of immigrants came by plane via JFK Airport, and consisted of people from the Dominican Republic, China, Mexico, and Jamaica. There are Asians, Latin Americans, West Indians, and nearly all are people of color. New York City is being remade again by a new wave of immigrants.

Like most cities in the northeastern United States and the Midwest, the population of New York City began to fall after 1950 as part of the great migration to the south and the west that took place in the United States. But unlike most of the cities losing population in that era, New York City stabilized around the 1980s, and by 1998 its population was back to 95 percent of its 1950 level. It exceeded all prior census years when it went back over eight million in 2000. New York City lost many residents to the great migration in the United States as did other cities, but new immigrants have replaced many of them.

The story of New York City is a microcosm of the United States. The population of the United States continues to grow, unlike that of many other western countries, because of the heavy immigration into the United States. And that same immigration flow produces a new population mix every year.

November 25, 1999 — Fishermen found a small five-year old boy cling-
ing to an inner tube three miles off the coast of Florida near Fort Laud-
erdale. It turned out that a small aluminum boat carrying 14 would-be
Cuban immigrants and the operator of the boat, a man residing in Miami
who smuggled Cubans into the United States for money, had capsized on its
way to Miami. The boat had a faulty engine, and only three survivors were
able to complete the journey to Florida on inner tubes. One of the survivors was five-year-old Elian Gonzalez (he turned six in December), and
in the next seven months he became world-famous in a struggle between
his Florida relatives and his father, who lived in and was a citizen of Cuba.

Elian's mother was romantically involved with the operator of the
boat, and they were both lost at sea in the tragedy. The Immigration and
Naturalization Service (INS) routinely paroled Gonzalez, as it did all
Cubans at the time who managed to reach the mainland of the United
States, but because of his age Elian was released to the custody of his great-
uncle, who lived in Miami. However, the father of Elian, now remarried,
had earlier called his Miami relatives to advise them that his ex-wife and
Elian had apparently left Cuba without his approval and to be on the
watch for them.

The Cuban community in Miami had no intention of returning
Elian, whose safe arrival they saw as sort of a miracle, but Elian's father
certainly was within his legal rights, even within International Law, to
demand the return of the boy who at only six years old was not legally eligible to make such a decision for himself. The result was a huge media
event for the next six months where the Cuban relatives generally had people's sympathies, but all objective advisors agreed the boy's father had all
the legal rights on his side, and public opinion polls generally stated the
boy should be returned to his father.

Analysts said probably the strongest public memory of the event was
the almost unbelievably clumsy way Attorney General Janet Reno and the
justice department handled the extraction of Elian from the house of his
Cuban relatives on April 22, 2000. A picture of a SWAT-team member of
the INS holding a huge machine-gun that was nearly as large as Elian who
had just emerged from hiding in a closet in a pre-dawn raid on the Miami
house in which Elian was staying made the front page of newspapers
around the world (and won a Pulitzer Prize for the photographer). It was

claimed later by many critics that the anger of the Miami Cuban community about how the event was handled by the Clinton administration cost Al Gore Florida's electoral votes in the razor-thin election in the fall of 2000, thus costing Gore the presidency.

The remainder of the Elian Gonzalez case after his extraction from Miami in April of 2000 was practically anti-climatic. Elian's father came to Washington, D.C., to stay with Elian until all legal appeals were exhausted. On June 1, 2000, the 11th United States Circuit Court of Appeals ruled that Elian was too young to file for asylum (only his father could speak for him) and that the Cuban relatives lacked legal standing to intervene. The United States Supreme Court refused to review the decision, and on June 28, 2000, Elian and his father returned home to Cuba to a hero's welcome.

This was quite a different result from that of a teenage Russian boy named Walter Polovchak 20 years earlier when the United States government did all it could to aid the boy to remain in the United States against the wishes of his parents (see entry for July 1980). But 20 years earlier the Cold War was still raging and the boy in question was a pawn in a much bigger game, immigration rules notwithstanding.

2000— The Congress passed yet another bill to assist illegal immigrants in gaining legal status. The bill was called the Legal Immigration and Family Equity Act even though it was aimed at illegal immigrants. The act granted the right to residency to about 400,000 illegal immigrants. It restored amnesty eligibility to specified illegal immigrants who had failed to apply under the 1986 Act (see entry for November 6, 1986), and also allowed illegal immigrants who were spouses or children of Americans to apply for residency while living in the United States instead of returning to their home country first.

The act was another lesson for illegal immigrants to do everything possible to get into the United States by any means, and then to bide their time waiting for a session of Congress to issue an amnesty of some sort. Further, the act would be referred to by illegal immigrants during Congressional debates in 2006–07 when proposals were made with a straight face to require illegal immigrants to return to their country of origin and pay hefty fines and other costs to be permitted to come back to the United

States and start a new path towards legality. Critics pointed out then that the 2000 act inferred that a simpler path would eventually appear for the illegal immigrants if they simply waited "in situ."

Another 2000 action that boded well for illegal immigrants was the declaration by the Executive Council of the American Federation of Labor/Congress of Industrial Organizations (AFL/CIO) that it supported blanket amnesty for illegal immigrants and it opposed nearly all attempts to sanction employers who hired them. This statement reversed Labor's traditional opposition to immigrants in general on the basis that they tended to lower wages.

However, there was more to this action than met the eye because a great schism was taking place within the AFL/CIO where the older industrial unions, losers of union membership for nearly 50 years, were competing for leadership with the newer service unions, which represented the only membership growth area within the AFL/CIO. The service unions saw illegal immigrants as a potential pool of new members rather than a threat to the wage scale, and the service unions were pressing for new union leadership and threatening to leave the AFL/CIO if it were not forthcoming.

The new AFL/CIO embrace of illegal immigrants reflected this battle within the labor establishment. In essence, many observers claimed, organized labor had crossed the line so many groups had crossed before them, i.e., they were no longer drawing a distinction between immigrants and illegal immigrants. Almost unnoticed, the battle in the United States over immigration was coming down to the issue of legal immigration versus illegal immigration, with proponents of illegal immigration trying to blur the line as much as possible to take advantage of the inherent positive feeling most Americans had towards legal immigration.

September 11, 2001— The infamous terrorist attacks of this date caused a detailed review of immigration policies far more intense than would ever have resulted from bursts of rhetoric in Congress. These attacks demonstrated that there were serious downsides to a dysfunctional immigration policy, especially when it was learned that the terrorists responsible for the attacks had easily entered the United States and worked together at different sites in the country without generating suspicion. All had easily obtained visas, and most terrorists were "standard" illegal immigrants who had simply stayed on when their visas expired. Subsequent immigration policy was forever changed after this date, beginning with the Patriot Act of October 2001 (see next entry).

The September 11, 2001, date marked the beginning of secular change in immigration policy. Nearly 100 years earlier the attitude towards immigration had changed from a laissez-faire approach to one that brought isolationist and restrictive immigration laws in the next three decades. These laws were somewhat relaxed after World War II, and then greatly liberalized in 1965 (see entry for October 2, 1965) even including the complications added by Displaced Persons, refugees, and immigrants claiming asylum. Nearly every change in the immigration laws after 1965 represented an attempt to accommodate ever more immigrants who desired to enter the United States. The watchword was compassion towards the less fortunate in the world.

However, the events of September 11, 2001, led to a series of laws where the prime watchword was security. There were many internal disputes in the United States between those who wanted more security and those who felt extra efforts must be made to be sure that the real or perceived civil rights of immigrants (including illegal immigrants) were protected even at the expense of security. Both laws defining the circumstances of admittance for immigrants and laws defining protocols for the deportation of illegal immigrants have been a matter of dispute, but laws and protocols emphasizing security have been winning out since 2001. Even the intended liberalization of immigration laws being pursued in Congress with a new Democratic majority in 2007 appear to have a chance of passing only if all work on a new fence along the border between the United States and Mexico and other security issues are completed before any liberalization in the proposed law are permitted to begin. The issue of security first now towers over any attempt to aid immigrants, especially illegal immigrants. This was expected to be the case for many years to come.

October 2001— President Bush officially created a new office of Homeland Security on October 8, and signed an antiterrorism bill known as the Patriot Act on October 26. These steps were the first of many intended to respond to the terrorist attacks of September 11, 2001. The Patriot Act provided additional resources for border control agents, and authorized the indefinite detention of any aliens suspected of engaging in terrorist activities. The attorney general was given discretion to determine who was a suspected terrorist. The Department of Justice had already detained several thousand individuals from the Middle East following the September 11, 2001, attacks. Federal immigration courts held closed hearings on their status, and those found to be in the country illegally were ordered deported.

Immigration Rights activists protested the closed hearings, only the beginning their complaints about the Patriot Act. From this date onward, immigration would be considered a national security issue. The fact that immigration had become essentially a "Civil Rights" issue in 1965 meant that future years would be filled with conflicts between the rights of the government to act in the defense of the country, versus what some persons saw as violations of basic civil rights.

November 25, 2002— President Bush signed legislation making the Department of Homeland Security a cabinet-level department (DHS). The Immigration and Naturalization Service (INS) was abolished (effective March 1, 2003) and its functions transferred from the Justice Department to the DHS. To some extent, the only real change was that the workforce that made up the INS now got their paychecks from the DHS. There was, however, a split of the administrative and enforcement duties once held by the INS. Within the DHS, there was a Bureau of Customs and Border Protection, a Bureau of Immigration and Customs Enforcement, and a Bureau of Citizenship and Immigration Services. This latter change meant one organization had responsibility for handling applications for visas, citizenship, asylum, and refugee status without at the same time having to worry about enforcement issues.

The real change was in the focus on immigration as a national security issue, but as always memories are short, and many members of Congress would soon return to their normal mindset where immigration was concerned and try to out do each other in attempting to further liberalize immigration laws. However, the effect of September 11, 2001, was that there were now be a more organized bloc of members of Congress who not only opposed such further liberalization, but who wanted to create restrictions on immigrants, especially illegal immigrants.

2004

August 3, 2004— The Statue of Liberty reopened nearly two years after having been closed due to the September 11, 2001, terrorist attacks. Extensive security and safety upgrades had been felt necessary before the national park could be re-opened to visitors.

October 1, 2004— A group called the Minuteman Project Inc. was founded by Jim Gilchrist of Aliso Viejo, California. Taking its name from the Minutemen who fought in the American Revolution in 1776, the group was a self-described "citizen's vigilance operation" attempting to reduce illegal immigration across the borders of the United States.

The group monitored sections of the border and advised the United States Border Patrol of any illegal activity it spotted. Further, the group has helped private landowners with properties at the border to build fences to protect against illegal immigrants. The group also engaged in political protest and similar activities to raise awareness of its mission. Almost by definition the group is controversial, but it has stimulated the formation of a separate group called the Minuteman Civil Defense Corps of Arizona, a similar operation trying to stem the tide of illegal immigrants into Arizona.

The Minuteman Project has been disparagingly called "vigilantes" by President Bush and praised as doing a "terrific job" by Arnold Schwarzenegger, governor of California. Public opinion about the group depends on personal feelings about immigrants in general and illegal immigrants in particular. The group has been involved in a long list of incidents since its founding in 2004, being granted credit or blame depending on the view about illegal immigrants held by the person reporting the incident. Some analysts say that at a minimum, the Minuteman demonstrates the frustration many people feel at being told only the federal government can act on immigration matters while Congress is unable to agree on any meaningful immigration actions, especially with respect to illegal immigration.

May 11, 2005— The Real ID Act of 2005 created additional restrictions on political asylum, curtailed habeas corpus relief for immigrants, increased immigration enforcement techniques, changed the judicial review process, and added federal restrictions to the issuing of state driver's licenses to immigrants and others. Because driver's licenses are universally used in the

United States as a form of identification, and are easily obtained illegally in many states, the federal restrictions were meant to develop a standard system for controlling them. This act was an example of how meaningful restrictions were being placed on immigrants, especially illegal immigrants, now that the Department of Homeland Security (DHS) was involved in the immigration process.

July 25, 2005 — The Teamsters and the Service Employees International Union declared that they were pulling out of the AFL-CIO overall union organization to form their own coalition. The United Food and Commercial Workers followed suit on July 29.

Among many other issues, the approach towards illegal immigrants was quite different between the "old" AFL-CIO unions and the new coalitions. Hispanics, legal and illegal, made up the bulk of the newer service-oriented unions. They saw illegal immigrants primarily as a source of new members, and thus viewed them in a positive light. The older traditional unions saw illegal immigrants as a source of downward pressure on wages and viewed them in a negative light. The AFL-CIO had officially changed their views on illegal immigrants to try to avoid just such a rupture, but other issues made the split almost inevitable.

December 16, 2005 — The House of Representatives passed a bill (H.R. 4437) that would make residing in the United States illegally a felony, and impose stiffer penalties on anyone knowingly employing and harboring non-citizens illegally. The bill also called for the construction of new fences along portions of the border between Mexico and the United States.

The bill proposed the toughest measures yet against illegal immigrants (far harsher than the controversial Prop 187 of 1994 — see entry for November 1994). A coalition of immigrant groups and those sympathetic to their cause carried out protests against the bill on March 25, 2006 (see entry), and urged the Senate not to agree to the House bill. This led to the May Day protests on May 1, 2006 (see entry). The fervor of the protests simply hardened the views of those in favor of the bill, most of whom were outraged that illegal immigrants would demonstrate in favor of their "right" to enter the United States illegally.

2006

2006— The third edition of *Immigrant America* was published by the University of California. The book, written by Alejandro Portes and Ruben G. Rumbaut, is a detailed and comprehensive history of immigration into the United States. As in the overwhelming majority of such books, the authors find immigration to be a very positive force in the history of the United States, and they generally disparage those who have opposed it at various points in the nation's history.

In the last paragraph of the book, the authors appeared to outdo themselves in criticizing recent events that apparently they find inappropriate to their view of immigration. In just that closing paragraph, they use the pejorative words "nativists, forced assimilationists, PULLAM advocates (the authors' coinage for pull the ladder after me), fearmongers, xenophobia, and restrictionism." The authors state all these recent negative issues will fail to prevent an immigration future "that mirrors the past."

The book was published in 2006, as noted, but these authors missed, as many others have, the clear split that was developing in the United States between attitudes towards legal as opposed to illegal immigration, a split that peaked between December of 2005 and the fall of 2007. There is a sort of arrogance implicit in resorting to name-calling to describe people whose view of immigration is different than your own, but for many years those who support immigration have used the word carelessly to include illegal immigration and have thus ignored (or in some cases hoped deliberately to obscure) the negative attitude building in the United States towards illegal immigration. All future immigration legislation will be hindered from proceeding until the nation is satisfied that solutions have been found to the problem of illegal immigration. Shrugging it off as a "perplexing problem" will no longer work. The issue of illegal immigration as of 2007 is now the prime issue in dealing with immigration.

March 9, 2006— One day before it expired, President Bush signed a renewal of the Patriot Act. The agreement on the renewal had been delayed by what had become a standard dispute between those espousing certain privacy rights and those urging tighter laws in what was essentially a new era of terrorism. Immigration per se was not an issue, but the flavor of the dispute was about to carry over into the immigration debate between those who favored traditional benefits for all immigrants and those who favored restrictions on illegal immigrants as a separate category in a new era of nearly unrestricted illegal immigration.

March 25, 2006— About 500,000 demonstrators in Los Angeles marched in protest against the immigration bill that had been passed by the House in 2005 (see entry for December 16, 2005) and was about to be considered by the Senate. Additional demonstrations were held elsewhere.

Beginning debate on March 29, the Senate basically rejected the House bill as being too harsh, and using a proposal known to be backed by President Bush, the Senate proposed a more lenient bill offering what became called a "path to citizenship" for millions of illegal immigrants. This proposal was considered simply "amnesty under another name" by backers of the House bill, and it seemed unlikely there would be a compromise reached on immigration legislation in 2006.

May 1, 2006— A nationwide boycott and demonstration in favor of both illegal and legal immigrants was held in cities across the United States (and in other countries as well). May 1 was picked as the day for the demonstrations because it is a regularly observed holiday in many countries, excluding the United States. The protest was called "Day Without Immigrants" in the United States to highlight the contributions immigrants made to the economy and to emphasize the need for more favorable immigration legislation.

The demonstrations had been planned in April as a follow-up to the demonstration in March (see previous entry) against the bill passed by the House of Representatives in 2005 (H.R. 4437, see entry for December 16, 2005) taking a tough stance on illegal immigration. The demonstrations were meant to protest once more against the House bill and support the more lenient Senate proposals made in March (see previous entry). Part of the House bill made illegal immigration a felony, and thus criminalized people in the immigrant community and elsewhere who provided support for illegal immigrants. Another part of this bill mandated construction of a fence across much of the border of the southwestern United States to deter illegal immigrants.

In a sense, the protests bore fruit because the Senate on May 25 passed a much more liberalized immigration bill even though polls across the United States indicated that most Americans favored tighter border security. Neither the House nor Senate bill was finalized in 2006 because neither side could convince the other of the desirability of its position. However, a "compromise" bill was passed on October 4, 2006 (see entry) that primarily addressed only the fence issue and gave members of Congress an opportunity to "go on the record" relative to immigration before the national elections in the fall.

News media across the country were full of self-congratulatory messages from the organizers of the so-called boycott. But as usual, there was another side to the nation's response to the May Day demonstrations that received much less publicity, and that may not bode well for those supporting illegal immigration as well as legal immigration.

There was general criticism of many marchers demanding their perceived rights in the United States while waving flags of Mexico and other South American countries. Also, a new group called the "You Don't Speak For Us" coalition was formed by Latinos pointing out that the May 1 demonstrators spoke only for themselves. Assistant Secretary of the Treasury Pete Nunez, spokesperson for the group, was quoted as saying: "Millions of Hispanic-Americans, including those who have gone through the immigration process the right way, are offended by the demands being made by people who have broken our nation's laws."

On an actions-speak-louder-than-words front, the Mayor and two council members were ousted May 2 in Herndon, Virginia, for previously supporting a day-labor center. The consensus by the *Washington Post* was that a negative reaction to the May Day activities sealed their fate. The *Post* also counted the Arizona legislature as an example of several state legislatures passing harsher laws against illegal immigrants as a backlash to the May 1 boycott. Further, President Bush announced plans on May 15 for the Pentagon to deploy up to 6,000 National Guard troops to help secure the southern border of the United States.

Analysts said that one result of the May Day demonstrations was to sharpen the distinction in the minds of many people between legal immigrants (which are generally supported) and illegal immigrants (which are becoming more and more strongly opposed). Congress will have a difficult time bridging this gap in immigration legislation of any sort. (As a footnote it should be added that the May Day demonstrations of 2007 (see entry for May 1, 2007) were only a pale imitation of those of 2006.)

August 22, 2006— The *Washington Post* carried a story about how the mayor of Hazleton, Pennsylvania, a small city of about 31,000 in the coal country of the northeastern corner of the state, was leading an effort to rid his city of illegal immigrants. He had sponsored an act approved by the City Council that would bar landlords from renting to illegal immigrants and revoke the business license of any business that hires an illegal immigrant.

The act faced the usual fate of such acts of being found unconstitutional by the courts, if only on the grounds that the federal government alone has the authority to regulate immigration (see entry for 1849), even though in recent years the Congress has had great difficulty in deciding how to do so. Other Constitutional objections to such acts beyond the 14th Amendment (see entry for July 28, 1868) include the problems involved with deciding who is and who is not an illegal immigrant. Hazleton is within easy reach of New York City, and many Puerto Ricans (who are in fact citizens of the United States) and immigrants from the Dominican Republic (many of whom claim legal asylum) have moved to Hazleton to find lower living expenses. Hazleton has tarred both groups with the illegal immigrant brush in the crackdown.

An organization called the Federation for American Immigration Reform (FAIR) said that one has to be very careful to be sure that their definition of the term illegal immigrant corresponds to federal immigration classifications. Otherwise legal steps will be taken to overturn anti-illegal immigrant acts (a Federal Judge would later issue a restraining order blocking the Hazleton act in November and plan more hearings on the issue. Onlookers then predict a very busy time in the courts for the Hazleton issue and others like it).

The legal details of the case are not the issue here per se, and the purpose of this chronology is not to track its resolution in the courts. Rather the purpose is to note that more and more state and local governments in the United States are trying to stop local problems they feel are brought on by illegal immigrants. Last year New Hampshire police chiefs began arresting illegal immigrants for trespassing, an approach ultimately stopped by the courts. Suffolk County on Long Island is planning to prohibit contractors from hiring illegal immigrants. The state of Arizona is carefully planning actions that will pass legal muster in attempting to control the impact of illegal immigrants in their state. At the other end of the spectrum, some cities in California have declared themselves "sanctuaries" for illegal immigrants. Many analysts say illegal immigration is a subject without an apparent middle ground.

October 4, 2006— President Bush signed a compromise immigration bill, which had managed to pass both the Senate and the House by dropping many of the harsher parts of the original house bill. The pressure of the upcoming fall elections helped to pass the compromise bill because many members of Congress wanted to be "on the record" concerning immigration.

The compromise bill authorized the construction of a 700-mile, double layered fence along the border between Mexico and the United States. But the Senate, as it has done so often with respect to immigration, passed that part of the bill with a "wink and a nod," deliberately excluding enough funds to finally complete the fence. The Democrats hoped to be big winners in the elections in November of 2006 (which they were) and thus be able to generate another liberalized immigration bill in 2007. But there was a strong bloc of votes in Congress opposed to yet another immigration bill that they felt would encourage more illegal immigration (the most recent estimate of the number of illegal immigrants in the United States was 11 million, up from 8.7 million in 2000 and climbing rapidly towards 12 million), and this bloc would be hard to overcome regardless of a new Democratic majorities in Congress in 2007.

November 14, 2006— The City Council of Farmer's Branch, Texas, a suburb of Dallas, became the first city in Texas to pass tough measures against illegal immigrants. The fate of the measures in the courts is still to be decided, just as for the ordinances passed in Hazleton, Pennsylvania (see entry for August 22, 2006), but in the same way as noted for the Hazleton issues, the purpose of including the Hazleton and Farmer's Branch items in this chronology is not to track them to their resolutions in the courts, but to demonstrate how local (and state) governments were trying to take actions at their level against illegal immigrants at this time.

The six City Council members voted unanimously to approve fines for landlords who rent to illegal immigrants, to make English the official language of the city, and to permit local authorities to screen suspects in police custody to check their immigration status. Notably, the council declined to vote on a proposal to penalize businesses that employ illegal immigrants. Like most states with high numbers of illegal immigrants, many businesses (and individuals) in Texas count on the low wages they can pay illegal immigrants while officially deploring their presence.

The action by the City Council made Farmer's Branch one of more than 50 municipalities nationwide that have considered, passed, or rejected similar anti-illegal immigrant laws. But Farmer's Branch is the first city to do so in the state of Texas, a haven for illegal immigrants for decades because they can easily cross the Rio Grande, the river that often runs very shallow as it marks the official border between Texas and Mexico. And jobs are always waiting for them in both the public and private sector.

December 7, 2006— Bill Richardson, Governor of New Mexico, told an audience at George Washington University in Washington, D.C., that the compromise immigration bill recently signed by President Bush (see entry for October 4, 2006) will not do much to solve the nation's illegal immigration problem because it concentrates only on building a fence between Mexico and the United States. Richardson feels a fence will simply place more strains on the system elsewhere, and it does not address the estimated 45 percent of illegal immigrants who enter the United States legally and then simply overstay their visas.

Richardson has unusually high credibility on the illegal immigration issue because he is a governor of a border state. During his tenure he declared a state of emergency in New Mexico and assigned the National Guard to patrol the border with Mexico. But Richardson is a liberal Democrat (with a Hispanic mother) who was expected to (and did) run for the Democratic nomination for president beginning in 2007. Thus, he brings issues from both sides of the table to the immigration debate. As governor of the most heavily Hispanic state in the nation, he has his finger on the pulse of Hispanic voters, but he speaks about the need for immigration reform for the nation as a whole, not just for immigrants. And he is definitely outspoken about the need to fix illegal immigration.

December 13, 2006— A news conference was held in Washington, D.C., by Homeland Security Secretary Michael Chertoff emphasizing the need to focus on workplaces to find employers who are hiring illegal immigrants and thus breaking the law in the United States. The news conference was held the day after raids were carried out on six meatpacking plants operated by Swift and Company in Denver, Colorado.

A total of 1,300 workers were detained on suspicion of providing stolen Social Security numbers to prove they were not illegal immigrants when they were hired. But four years before, when the company pressed the need for workers to provide proof they were in the country legally, the company ended up being fined $200,000 for discrimination.

The situation emphasized the difficulties companies faced in meeting all government regulations pertaining to hiring workers when the government agencies themselves can not agree on how to implement their many regulations. Just last summer the Department of Homeland Security (DHS) proposed a rule to ease the problem of verifying Social Security numbers, but the Equal Opportunity Commission warned DHS that the proposed rule could result in violations of nondiscrimination laws. The DHS proposal was put on hold.

This problem is typical of so many immigration rules regarding illegal immigrants. "Everyone" agrees "something" must be done about illegal immigrants, but no one seems to be able to find a something that would be effective without running afoul of the multitude of often conflicting regulations meant to protect workers, especially low-wage workers, in the United States. That makes the problem of writing immigration laws even more daunting.

December 31, 2006— Data released later would show that 1,266,264 immigrants entered the United States legally during the year of 2006. This was the largest number of new immigrants to enter the United States since the record year of 1907 (see entry for December 31, 1907) when 1,285,349 entered the country legally. The years of 1990 and 1991 show bigger numbers on the register (about 0.3 million and 0.6 million more respectively), but these were mainly made up of illegal immigrants who received amnesty per the 1986 law (see entry for November 6, 1986) and were finally counted in the totals (as "adjustments") for 1990 and 1991 (and other years). Those receiving amnesty had been in the United States for years, and the only thing "new" about them was that they were now officially being counted.

Supporters of immigrants like to use the 1990 and 1991 numbers as "proof" that the United States is not presently being overrun with immigrants. But it is a "proof" similar to nearly all things involved with immigration. Both sides twist all numbers as necessary to support their position. Actually, the number of truly new arrivals to the United States has remained nearly constant at about an annual total of 400,000 from 1986 to the present. The average annual total over that period exceeds 900,000 per year. Thus, the number of "adjustments" is higher annually than for "pure" newcomers for that period. Nothing about immigration data is as simple as it seems at first glance.

It is estimated that the near-record total in 2006 may have been as much as 35 percent higher if illegal immigrants were also counted. But no one actually knows how many illegal immigrants enter the United States each year, and similarly nobody actually knows how many illegal immigrants are presently in the United States. There is general agreement that there were about 12 million illegal immigrants in the United States as of 2007. But no matter how often the number is used in many emotion debates, it is only a guess.

January 10, 2007 — California's two Democratic Senators, Dianne Feinstein and Barbara Boxer, presented a bill calling for a "blue card" for agricultural workers to bring in the harvest of California farmers. It is estimated that about one million illegal immigrants work on the 76,500 farms in California, making up about 90 percent of the agricultural payroll in the state. Many illegal immigrants are leaving seasonal agricultural work for better-paying jobs in the construction, restaurant, and hospital industries. About three or four billion dollars could be lost from California's $34 billion dollars a year agricultural industry if enough workers can not be found at harvest time.

The proposal was made together with many backers of the bill attending the news conference. The proposal was seen as having enough votes to pass the Senate, but all backers said they would prefer to make the bill part of a larger immigration package. The bill would offer benefits to seasonal workers in that it would permit travel back-and-forth between Mexico and the United States, and after the five year period of the bill, it would offer permanent legal residence in the United States to workers meeting certain conditions.

The bill would revamp the H-2A guest worker program, which is described as a "bureaucratic thicket" requiring farmers to go through 60 different steps to get workers from abroad. Only two percent of American agriculture uses the plan because it is so difficult to use, and that has led to the use of illegal immigrants to harvest crops, according to the National Council of Agricultural Employers.

Analysts say it is very difficult to hire workers on a seasonal basis in any business, and hiring them fulltime to do only seasonal work would not make economic sense in any industry. If the product is perishable as it is in agriculture, the problem is even more acute. The problem has existed for many decades and did not suddenly arise in the era of illegal immigration. Basically, "guest worker" programs have existed for many years as the economy of the United States constantly expanded. There will be more of the same in the future, and all immigration bills will have to address this issue.

February 5, 2007— A report showed that the number on inmates in the jails of Los Angeles County who may be illegal immigrants rose from 3,050 in 2005 to 5,829 in 2006. This increase is not attributed to any increase per se in the number of illegal immigrants being arrested, but rather to an improved and more intensive screening program.

It was (and still is) the policy of the county not to inquire into the resident status of people who could be possible witnesses to crime on the basis that such inquiries could keep immigrants from coming forward to report criminal activity. But a change was made in the case of persons already arrested for a crime and in custody. It was felt this would a very small effect on the community at large, and if people already in custody were illegal immigrants, they were subject to deportation after serving time for their crimes.

Federal agents were called in to help local personnel in their screening work, and to do some screening on their own. Federal officials estimate that about 40,000 of the 170,000 inmates who pass through Los Angeles County jails annually (a rate of 24 percent) are in the United States illegally. Lee Baca, the Sheriff of Los Angeles County, praised the improved screening program, and hoped to improve it.

February 14, 2007— It was reported by the *Wall Street Journal* that Bank of America, one of the largest banks in the United States, had just expanded to 51 branches in Los Angeles its program of offering credit cards to customers with no Social Security numbers and no formal credit histories (the program was started in 2006 in five locations). Such a category of customers would, of course, include illegal immigrants. Some commentators have criticized Bank of America for its relatively new policy and have suggested such programs offer terrorists more ways for money laundering.

The program is less open-ended than it seems because Bank of America offers it only to checking account customers whose accounts are in good standing. In this way the bank does have a good credit history on the customers it deals with. The amounts of credit offered are relatively small, and the interest rates relatively high. These facts alone explain why the bank is interested in this kind of business, which could provide relatively high profit margins.

However, the bank has broader horizons in mind. It has recognized the growing number of Hispanics in its market area, and has been active in helping checking customers remit money back to their home country by eliminating various transfer fees. The bank also actively deals in opening bank accounts and supplying such financial products as mortgages. Its new credit card programs are seen as a way to help its customers build credit histories, and as Los Angeles leads the nation in the number of Latino-owned firms (as well as Asian-owned firms), the Bank of America feels it is establishing early business relationships with the successful entrepreneurs of tomorrow. Whatever the outcome of the newest immigration bill, the Bank recognizes that Hispanics are here to stay in the Los Angeles area, and if the bank doesn't grow in the Hispanic area, it doesn't grow at all. Immigration is immigration, but business is business.

February 20, 2007 — An article in the *Wall Street Journal* about Bank of America offering credit cards to customers with no Social Security numbers (see previous entry) brought forth a spate of articles about other financial organizations doing the same thing for established customers.

A nonprofit worker center in New Jersey called New Labor, which helps immigrants learn English, last November became the first organization in the nation to offer the "Sigo" card (combining "yes" in Spanish with the word "go"). The center has distributed only 300 cards so far (the card is affiliated with MasterCard), but the program is underway at eight other worker centers in the United States, including the Filipino Worker Center and the Institute of Popular Education of Southern California, both in Los Angeles. Organizers hope to expand it to a total of 160 such centers serving thousands of immigrants.

Other banks do offer banking and credit card services similar to the worker centers, including the aforementioned Bank of America and Wells Fargo. The worker centers claim to offer lower fees. The point to consider, however, is that there are plenty of sources offering banking services to immigrants, including illegal immigrants, if one takes the trouble to seek them out.

February 26, 2007— The nearly frenzied media hunt for banks providing financial services for immigrants, including illegal immigrants, triggered by recent news articles (see entries for February 14, 2007, and February 20, 2007) finally reached the top, so to speak. It was "discovered" that the Federal Reserve Bank has had a program operating for four years dubbed Directo a Mexico that operates in conjunction with the Central Bank of Mexico.

The program makes it easier for Mexican nationals in the United States to send money to Mexico. It started following a meeting between President Bush and then–Mexican President Fox in 2003. The program is perfectly legal in all ways, and it complies with the Patriot Act by requiring identification with a picture ID (such as a consular identification card) which is regularly checked by the bank for authenticity. The media "discovered" that such identification methods legally exclude Social Security cards, which make it possible for immigrants (even illegal immigrants) without Social Security cards to participate in such programs.

The media, being the media, always headlines the issue that no Social Security cards are required and gathers quotes from persons known to be opposed to anything to do with illegal immigrants to give the appearance that the media has unearthed some nefarious scheme or conspiracy. Actually, in all these financial institution stories, all applicable laws are being scrupulously followed, and there is no story where the media desperately wants to have a story. The point is that the lack of a Social Security card does not prove a person is in the United States illegally, especially when they have other means of identification. The media knows this, but a story is a story.

February 27, 2007— Texas State Representative Leo Berman was the focus of a story outlining how the state of Texas, long a haven for illegal immigrants because of the ease with which Mexican immigrants have routinely crossed the border (1,300 miles long) with Texas to find work, was attempting to pass legislation to bar illegal immigrants from receiving certain benefits in the United States. Berman was concentrating on the way the 14th Amendment automatically gives citizenship to all children born in the United States. The issue has been affirmed before, and is not one states can legislate (only the federal government can do so), but Berman admits his goal is to set off a battle in the Federal Courts to re-consider the issue.

There is little chance Berman will succeed, but his legislation is only one of a number of proposals essentially attacking illegal immigrants in Texas in a reversal of prior history. According to the National Conference of State Legislatures, in 2006 a total of 570 immigration measures were proposed with 84 being signed into law. The Conference predicts immigration will be a "hot button" issue again in 2007, showing once more how important (and difficult) it will be to find common ground on any immigration bill finally proposed by Congress.

February 28, 2007— Homeland Security Secretary Michael Chertoff launched a high-profile effort to build support for the 2007 immigration reform being considered by Congress when he testified at the first Capitol Hill hearings on immigration since the Democrats took over Congress in the 2006 elections.

Chertoff worked quietly to build support for the bill, and led a helicopter tour for several members of Congress to view the progress being made on the fence being built on the border with Mexico in San Luis, Arizona. In a news conference held the day before, Chertoff told reporters that the administration wanted to work closely with Congress to get a bill that would address everyone's concerns, but in a way that would finally end in the passage of a bill. The bottom line of government according to Chertoff is "to get stuff done."

2007

March 1, 2007—During this week Colorado officials announced in Denver that they hope to start a pilot program this month using convicts to harvest crops rather than the illegal immigrants often used. Ever since the Colorado Legislature passed what were advertised as the toughest laws in the nation against illegal immigration last summer, labor shortages have occurred as immigrants, both legal and illegal, have been leaving the state.

The "tough" legislation included the need for state identification to get government services, and permission for police to check the immigration status of persons suspected of committing crimes. The prisoners who will work in the fields will be low-security prisoners who volunteer to work for 60 cents a day and possible bonuses. The farmers who contract for the inmates will have to pay for associated prison guards, and the total costs — yet to be negotiated — are expected by farmers to exceed the costs of their traditional workers. But at least the crops will get picked.

Farmers met with state officials on Monday to discuss using inmate labor, and the Department of Corrections expects to start sending about 100 prisoners to work on farms near Pueblo later this month. The program highlights the need for an improved guest worker section in a new immigration bill expected to be debated in a few months in Congress.

March 1, 2007 — Valley Park— The town of Valley Park, Missouri, became once again highlighted among the growing list of places in the United States that have passed local laws or ordinances against illegal immigrants. St. Louis County Circuit Judge Barbara Wallace was to hear oral arguments this day on the validity of the most recent version of Valley Park's attempt to bar landlords from renting to illegal immigrants. Newspapers like to headline such stories with comments about a new precedent possibly in the offing, but they know very well no such thing is likely to occur. The most probable occurrence is the scheduling of another hearing or an injunction that will cause Valley Park to draft yet another version of their ordinance and the struggle through the courts will continue.

As noted in the previous entries in this chronology regarding such community actions (see entries for August 22, 2006, and November 14, 2006), the intent of this listing is not to track the associated events through their almost endless sequence of court hearings, but rather to indicate the frequency of the attempted imposition of anti-illegal immigrant laws by individual communities as a result of what they see as continued inaction by the federal government in a area the courts continue to say only the federal government can act. The real sense of suspense in these actions is whether or not some community somewhere can develop an ordinance that passes Constitutional muster regarding illegal immigration. If so, a veritable flood of similar legislation is certain to follow across the United States. But such an event is many years off considering the glacial pace of court actions in the United States.

March 28, 2007 — Two executives of the Golden State Fence Company were sentenced in federal court in San Diego, California, after being found guilty of knowingly hiring illegal immigrants. United States District Judge Barry T. Moskowitz sentenced the executives to three years of probation, 180 days of home confinement, 1,040 hours of community service, and fines of $200,000 and $100,000 each. Further, the Company had to forfeit $4.7 million in profits earned from their employment of illegal immigrants.

Prosecutors had urged six months of jail time for the offenders, as the company had a prior history of being involved in such practices, but the Judge opted for probation because the company had treated the illegal immigrants fairly, including payment of equitable wages and benefits. Immigration and Customs Enforcement (ICE) had previously warned the Company as long ago as 1999 about hiring illegal immigrants, and in November of 2005 had executed search warrants and found violations to which the executives pleaded guilty in December of 2006.

The most notable thing about the case was that ICE had shown it was getting serious about enforcement of the law forbidding employers from knowingly hiring illegal immigrants. The law had been on the books since the amnesty of 1986 (see entry for November 6, 1986), but it had been a law "more honored in the breech than the observance." Michael Carney, acting special agent for ICE in San Diego, said, "this is the first criminal prosecution of an employer for violating hiring laws covering illegal immigrants in San Diego." Because San Diego is, and has been, a hotbed of illegal immigration for many years, that statement was confirmation of the non-prosecution of employers for hiring illegal immigrants.

According to ICE, there were only 25 arrests nationwide in 2002 for cases involving improper hiring of illegal immigrants and related charges. In 2006, there were 716. Carney hoped the increase would have an appropriate deterrent effect. But Mark Krikorian, Executive Director of the Center for Immigration Studies in Washington, D.C., a group that supports tighter immigration controls, said he believes the Bush administration was stepping up the enforcement of immigration laws to build political credibility with Congress to get them to approve a new amnesty bill. Krikorian said it was simply an obvious case of a "spoonful of enforcement will help the amnesty go down."

March 28, 2007 — Illinois — The Illinois House of Representatives approved a bill giving illegal immigrants a special permit to drive a car. An Illinois Senate committee approved a similar bill earlier this year, and Governor Rod Blagojevich has pledged to sign it, so the bill appears to have a very good chance of becoming law. If so, Illinois will join Hawaii, Maine, Maryland, Michigan, New Mexico, Oregon, and Washington as states granting driver's licenses without proof that the applicant is in the country legally.

The arguments on both sides of the issue have almost become clichés. Proponents claim illegal immigrants, who are driving anyway, will be encouraged to get insurance and take proper training. Opponents say giving driver's licenses to illegal immigrants is just another step in rewarding them for illegal behavior, and will simply attract more illegal immigrants and provide an additional avenue for terrorists to integrate themselves into American society. As in most arguments about illegal immigration, there is no middle ground. Illegal immigrants are either viewed as criminals deserving of no benefits, or as regular immigrants deserving of everyone's help. This is why the upcoming immigration bill will be so hard to reconcile between opposing viewpoints.

April 1, 2007 — As the first full week of legislative activity in Congress in April approached, it was confirmed by some individuals that members of the Bush administration had been meeting with key Senators of both parties to work out an immigration bill that would attract enough Republican Senators to pass a Senate bill that would be able to also pass in the House as well. Attempts were being made to avoid the partisan battles of

2006 when neither the House nor the Senate could develop a bill that the other side would even consider.

It was felt that both sides were in a "now or never" position in that president Bush favored what most Democrats wanted, i.e., a new version of amnesty for the estimated 12 million illegal immigrants already in the country, and if he could get enough improvements in greater effective border security (including new tools for the Department of Homeland Security to identify illegal immigrants), a deal could be worked out that would attract enough conservative Republicans (and Democrats) to pass a bill. No one knew what a new President and a new Congress would do in 2009 after being elected in late 2008. So the incentive to do something right now was very high.

April 5, 2007— Shannon O'Neill, a political science professor at Columbia University in New York who was writing a book on Mexico–United States relations had an article published containing demographic data that offered a completely different view on the issue of immigrants flowing across the border from Mexico to work in the United States. In O'Neill's view, the United States may soon have to find ways to entice Mexican workers (including illegal immigrants) to come rather than expending a great deal of energy finding ways to keep them out.

According to O'Neill, Mexican women are now averaging 2.2 births each, only slightly above the 2.1 rate applying in the United States. Life expectancy in Mexico has increased to 75 years, only slightly behind the 77 that applies in the United States. The result is that by 2050, Mexico's population distribution will be as old as that in the United States.

In the last ten years, nearly 5 million Mexicans have come to work in the United States. But the economically active population, which grew by more than one million members yearly in the 1990s, is now adding only 0.5 million annually, which means that in the next ten years five million fewer new workers will be available compared to the previous decade.

The United States in turn is facing a demographic downturn, especially with more people aiming at jobs requiring more education and leaving the lower tiers even emptier yet. This is actually another way of looking at the fact that most Western Nations are in a population decline with only the United States maintaining steady growth due to its desirability as an immigration target. O'Neill suggests that this means that any new immigration bill needs to find ways to legalize existing illegal immigrants and to provide a good guest-worker program as its major goals.

April 9, 2007 — President Bush unveiled key parts of his new immigration program in a speech in Yuma, Arizona. Speaking from a Border Patrol station, Bush gave few details of his new plan, but the key elements remained similar to a plan he proposed last year. However, there were more stringent requirements for existing illegal immigrants to gain citizenship and more mentions of the improved border fence work going on right before his eyes in Yuma. The major question is whether enough Republicans can be wooed with greater security efforts to accept the bitter pill of what they see as amnesty.

April 10, 2007 — John J. Sweeney, president of the AFL-CIO, wrote an article attacking the guest-worker concept of existing immigration law and urging changes in any upcoming version that may be written. Unions have generally opposed guest-worker programs on the grounds that such programs tend to lower existing wage scales, and even when unions changed their philosophy years ago of opposing immigration to one of acceptance, they still opposed guest-worker programs.

However, an interesting change has been taking place in recent years following the split between the AFL-CIO and unions that primarily consist of service workers. The service worker unions have been growing while the older unions represented by the AFL-CIO have continued their decades-long period of decline. The real basis of the split was that the old AFL-CIO no longer represents the needs of the new service unions. The service unions, whose membership in some cases is 80 percent immigrant, see guest-worker programs in terms on an opportunity to add more members. With their members already near the bottom of the wage scale, a general depression of wages is less of an issue for service workers who see a growing membership with growing clout as the best way to improve their working conditions.

Many analysts claim the union philosophy of accepting immigrants changed only when they realized new immigrants represented their best opportunity to reverse the long time membership decline in unions in general. Now that union leadership in the AFL-CIO has lost the support of the robust service unions, the AFL-CIO does not really speak for unions in general, and the "union" position on the guest-worker portion on any upcoming immigration bill depends on which unions one speaks to.

April 11, 2007 — Reports surfaced that a new lawsuit was being prepared to challenge the use of Special Order 40 that has been in use for more than three decades by the Los Angeles Police Department (LAPD) and subsequently by many police departments across the United States. Essentially Special Order 40 prevents the police from questioning immigrants about their legal immigration status when investigating a crime. The rationale is that if immigrants know such questions may come up, they will try to avoid cooperating with police investigations, including not reporting crimes in their neighborhoods.

Opponents of Special Order 40 and others like it claim it is just another instance of "coddling" illegal immigrants and tying the hands of the police. With a recent survey showing that 20 percent of all jail inmates in Los Angeles are illegal immigrants, opponents to Special Order 40 claim much more needs to be done to identify and arrest illegal immigrants.

The new lawsuit is supposed to be based on an obscure drug enforcement law requiring certain identifications of illegal immigrants involved in drug-related crimes (which are a large percentage of the total in large cities). But actually the legal basis for the suit and whether it is filed soon or not are basically irrelevant issues. If the suit happens it will of course go the courts, and the courts in today's world are places where non-federal lawsuits attempting to place restrictions on illegal immigrants go to die. The true relevance of the anticipated lawsuit to this chronology is that it shows once more the public anger over the apparent inability of anyone in the United States to deal with the problems caused by illegal immigration is an ever-growing anger needing resolution. Once more present conditions are increasing the stakes of coming up with a meaningful and effective immigration reform.

April 23, 2007 — A talk radio symposium began in Washington, D.C., and ran through April 27 to discuss the topics of immigration and especially illegal immigration. The various talk show hosts broadcast from a hotel meeting room while about 600 talk radio fans looked on at different times. The stated purpose of the event was to lobby Congress to take a hard line on immigration in general and on illegal immigration specifically. The radio hosts were all strongly opposed to any sort of amnesty, and they attacked President Bush and those Congressional supporters who spoke in favor of some sort of amnesty as part of any immigration bill.

April 25, 2007 — A hearing was held within the House of Representatives concerning the seemingly endless issue of the status of Puerto Rico. After being ceded to the United States following the Spanish-American War of 1898 (see entry for April 24, 1898), and then being declared citizens of the United States in 1917 by the Jones-Shafroth Act (see entry for March 2, 1917), some Puerto Rican citizens appear to be always seeking a change in status. Presently a commonwealth since the 1950s with limited voting rights in the United States government (and a correspondingly limited tax burden), there is an ongoing battle between those who want to become a full-fledged state and those who want to preserve the status quo (and a very small minority who want to become an independent country).

Four "unofficial" plebiscites were held in Puerto Rico after 1967, with a slight majority favoring the status quo. In the last plebiscite in 1998, several new options were presented and 50.3 percent of the voters choose "none of the above," with statehood winning 46.5 percent. Independence won less than three percent. The present hearing gave no indication that a definitive decision would be made anytime in the near future.

April 30, 2007 — Gregory Rodriguez, a well-known writer on immigration issues, wrote an article focusing on the situation in Colorado where a program has been established to use inmate labor to pick crops due to the shortage of illegal immigrants, a number of whom have fled the state because of its recent "get tough on illegal immigrants" legislation (see entry for March 1, 2007).

Rodriguez points out the basic problem has been going on for decades. Farmers want what he calls "indispensable, disposable" workers, i.e., skilled workers in terms of picking crops (which many are surprised to find demands a certain type of skill) who then leave after the crops have been picked. In essence, this is what a well-run guest worker program offers. If illegal immigrants are going to be eliminated in some way, a good guest worker program must exist or farmers are going to face labor shortages and crops are going to rot in the fields.

May 1, 2007— May Day protest marches in support of both illegal and legal immigrants were held across the United States and in other countries. But the marches were a pale imitation of those held in 2006 (see entry for May 1, 2006). If it were not for the familiar cries of police brutality when the police responded to the throwing of rocks and bottles by some fringe elements among the marchers near the end of the day in Los Angeles, the news of the marches would have faded very quickly. Even at that, most news reports of the various marches concluded that the organizers of such marches may have gone to the well once too often.

However, a small march of about 2,000 people in Los Angeles in response to the events of May Day was completed without incident on May 17. The marchers were orderly and the police equally so. Once again it was shown that such marches could be done successfully if the organizers can find ways to eliminate those among the marchers who are out for hooliganism rather than a cause.

May 10, 2007— Tamar Jacoby, a senior fellow at the Manhattan Institute, while launching a new nonprofit organization called Our Pledge designed to help immigrants become Americans, wrote an article concerning the latest developments surfacing about a new immigration bill and what kind of guest-worker program is needed in that bill.

Jacoby claimed that the new bill that has been worked on for several weeks "in a backroom on Capitol Hill" had resolved the contentious issue of amnesty. The new bill will offer a path to legalization to nearly all the estimated 12 million illegal immigrants in the country today, requiring a list of complicated steps that must be taken by illegal immigrants so that the deadly word "amnesty" can be properly camouflaged. Jacoby is highly in favor of this provision.

But Jacoby identifies the question of appropriate programs under which visas will be issued for additional immigrants and guest workers as an even more important issue in terms of defining what form immigration will take going forward. According to Jacoby, for many years the

United States has needed to issue an average of about 1.5 million visas to foreigners — workers and their families — to meet the needs of the economy. But we lack the political will to admit it, and only about 1 million visas are issued. The missing 0.5 million are filled primarily by illegal immigrants.

Initial information about the upcoming bill infers it contains a large guest-worker program of from 200,000 to 600,000 participants, and it includes provisions to admit new legal immigrants on a basis of "points" for job skills rather than just automatically giving top preference to family members. A contentious issue involves the question of whether or not guest workers can later find a path to legalization. The operative term is "temporary" means "temporary." Jacobs suggests admitting a wide array of foreign workers and then later using a point system to evaluate those who wish to stay.

May 17, 2007 — The Senate announced that a key group of Senators and persons from the Bush administration had come up with a proposed compromise immigration bill that addressed the problems of how to deal with the estimated 12 million illegal immigrants presently in the country and how to improve border security to reduce the number of illegal immigrants in the future. The proposed bill was to be introduced on the Senate floor in the next week for debate and amendments.

It was stressed that as in all compromises, there were many things in the bill that persons on all sides of the debate would dislike. However, it was also stressed that the window of opportunity for reaching agreement on some sort of substantive immigration bill was growing very narrow. After the summer of 2007, the members of Congress would turn their attention to the upcoming election year of 2008, and many could be reluctant to take a compromise position in an election year on such an emotional subject as illegal immigration. Further, President Bush, who strongly favors such a compromise, is "termed out" and thus forbidden to run again in 2008. If the new president takes a different view, a compromise that could overcome a possible presidential veto would be highly unlikely. Thus, the time to reach a compromise position is right now. All parties realized this situation when the year began, but time has passed without action for a number of reasons, and the deadline is now very much in the present tense.

The bill is definitely a compromise. Nearly all of the estimated 12 million illegal immigrants will be given the opportunity to apply for legal status over time, but the conditions applied do not lead automatically to legalization without the payment of various fines and fees and the requirement for heads of households to leave the United States and reapply for legal entry from their countries of origin. These conditions hopefully remove the taint of "amnesty" according to the Democrats. Further, none of the key provisions of the legalization process could begin until the border fence between the United States and Mexico is completed (about 18 months from now), and the number of border patrol agents has been substantially increased from the present 12,000 to 18,000. The Democrats hope this tightening of border security will get enough Republicans, who are fervently opposed to what they see as amnesty, to vote for the bill, especially when the security portions of the bill must be completed to "trigger" the legalization portions of the bill. But there are many Democrats opposed to portions of the bill involving a "Guest-Worker" program, and a change in emphasis on the admission of new immigrants based on a point score taking in to account the skills and education of new immigrants rather than automatically giving preference solely to the reunification of families.

Thus, as noted, there are many things for everyone to dislike about the proposed legislation. Agreeing on a compromise bill requires finding common ground to work from, and a subject as emotional as illegal immigration may not have a common ground. The next several weeks of debate will determine if one can be established in the existing Congress.

May 25, 2007 — The end of the first week of debate on the proposed immigration bill in the Senate (just before Congress took its traditional two week break for Memorial Day) was very encouraging to those members of the Senate and the Bush administration who had crafted together the compromise bill being debated. There had been no proposed amendments passed that were felt to endanger the future of the compromise, and the one close vote on the issue of skilled immigrant workers was resolved in favor of those trying to shepherd the bill through the Senate. There was general optimism that the legislation would now eventually pass the Senate and move on to a tough period of debate in the House.

2007

June 3, 2007 — Newspapers across the United States were full of stories about the group of Senators (and some Bush administration personnel) who had gotten together over the past few months to put together the compromise immigration bill presently being debated in the Senate. All stories emphasized the sense of bipartisanship that had resulted in the "Grand Bargain" that had evolved from months of effort.

Some analysts pointed out that regardless of the specific detail in the 626-page bill, what was truly unique about the bill was the approach used to get the support of enough members of Congress to pass it. Rather than try to carve off a little here and a little there as is the case in most contentious bills needing lots of compromise, the authors of the bill had basically included all the key elements both the Democrats and Republicans insisted be in the bill. Thus, each side had a prime reason to vote for the bill instead of simply voting against the bill to keep the other side from gaining an edge in what they wanted.

The Democrats were most interested in gaining some sort of amnesty for a large number of the estimated 12 million illegal immigrants already in the country. The bill as written proposed a path to legalization for nearly all the illegal immigrants presently here. The terms were complicated and far from automatic in a way that hopefully would reduce the bitterness of the taste of any sort of amnesty the Republicans would feel.

The Republicans were anxious to build their security fence and other controls on the Mexican border, and to give the Department of Homeland Security (DHS) more tools to find illegal immigrants presently in the country. The bill gave the Republicans what they wanted in these areas, and, in addition, stated that these security issues must be completed first before any of the amnesty-related issues could begin.

The other key issues regarding the details of a guest worker program and changing preferences for standard new visas from primarily family reunification to a mix of criteria including the job skills and education of the new applicant hopefully could be worked out in a spirit of compromise to get the total bill passed.

What was unique about the process used to present the bill was that a group of Senators got together to agree on the terms of the bill (after much debate) and then agreed to vote as a bloc for the bill even if they personally disagreed with certain issues. They also agreed to work together on the Senate floor to help shepherd the bill through tight votes and derail any proposed amendments that might make the bill come apart before passage. Help from the Bush administration was a key in putting the process together, but this angle was pushed into the background once the key Senators announced the bill.

The "Gang of 12" that played the key role in the Senate were Edward Kennedy (D–Massachusetts), Dianne Feinstein (D–California), John Kyl (R–Arizona), Mel Martinez (R–Florida), Arlen Specter (R–Pennsylvania), Johnny Izakson (R–Georgia), Lindsey Graham (R–South Carolina), Ken Salazar (D–Colorado), Saxby Chambliss (R–Georgia), Richard Durbin (D–Illinois), Patrick Leahy (D–Vermont), and Charles Schumer (D–New York). Actually, the number changed somewhat depending on the issue being discussed. John Cornyn of Texas and Robert Menendez of New Jersey were heavily involved during the process, but finally broke with the group over specific issues they would not agree to vote for at the end. Homeland Security Secretary Michael Chertoff and Commerce Secretary Carlos M. Gutierrez had a lot to do with reaching out from the White House to a bring the key group of Senators together to avoid a repeat of the 2006 process that failed to produce a comprehensive immigration bill both the Senate and House could even come close to reaching an agreement upon.

Observers cautioned that even though the approach to drafting and presenting the bill was unique, there was no assurance enough of a common ground existed to actually get an immigration bill passed in this session of Congress, no matter how high the sense of urgency extended.

June 7, 2007 — The highly touted "grand bargain" immigration bill came to a halt in the Senate tonight when Majority Leader Harry Reid pulled the bill from the Senate floor as he was unable to win a vote to cut off debate and stop the seemingly endless string of amendments being proposed to the basic bill (at last count 42 amendments had been acted upon and there was no agreement as to how many more would be forthcoming). As in most everything in Washington, D.C., party politics triumphed over all other factors. Reid, a Democrat, was seen as trying to bluff Republicans, who were proposing most of the amendments and refusing to agree on a limit of 10–12 more, into cutting off the debate by threatening to pull the bill off the floor. The bluff failed and Reed was thus forced to pull the bill. As he did, the blame game moved into high gear.

Reed's claim of the need to move on to more pressing business was somewhat blunted by the fact that the next piece of business he wanted to schedule was a vote of no confidence in controversial attorney general Alberto Gonzalez, a purely political stunt that had no effect in law and that would only waste time in the Senate, if it came to a vote at all (which it did not). Reid further took advantage of the attendance of President Bush at a worldwide economic conference in Europe to say it was the failure of the President to apply more pressure on balking Republicans to get the bill through the Senate.

The legislation was filled with many complex issues that were being debated in the Senate, but the word was that the issue on which the most mail and phone calls were being received by the Senate members was that of what was seen as amnesty. Americans by the millions were highly opposed to giving illegal immigrants any kind of amnesty, no matter what kind of provisions or criteria were attached to give the illusion that "pure" amnesty was not involved. The basic problem seemed to be not so much the concept of some kind of legalization but the belief that the government would not follow through on its promises of much tighter enforcement of security issues before beginning legalization of any kind.

Supporters of the bill vowed to bring it back to the Senate floor for further debate, but immigration reform was proving to be as emotional an issue as ever. The feeling was deepening in many places that if the present bill could not be retrieved, future immigration legislation may turn only in the direction of more enforcement and even criminalization of existing illegal immigrants, as had the legislation passed by the House at the end of 2005 (see entry for December 16, 2005).

June 13, 2007 — Jorge G. Castaneda, a former foreign minister of Mexico, who is now a professor of politics and Latin American studies at New York University, wrote an article commenting on the pending immigration that illegal immigrants had be coming north from Mexico (and countries south of it) at a rate of about 500,000 per year. Further, this rate would continue for at least the next ten years.

Castaneda said the key issues in any immigration package were how to deal with the illegal immigrants already here, and the Temporary Worker Program (TWP). He pointed out that any TWP should attempt to issue legal visas in an amount that would at least outnumber the number of illegal immigrants. Otherwise, the inference was, the number of illegal immigrants would simply continue to grow in the future.

Much of what Castaneda had to say was not new from the Mexican point of view, but some observers noted that at least Castaneda was confirming in writing the large numbers of illegal immigrants constantly flowing into the United States, and Castaneda was in a unique position to know whereof he spoke.

June 14, 2007 — A group of Senators confirmed that the immigration bill would return to the Senate floor for further debate as early as next week, with a goal of completing a bill by the end of June. A key action was a promise by President Bush to pursue separate funding for the security measures in the immigration bill to insure that these measures would be fully funded at the beginning of the bill and not be subject to the normal Congressional second guessing in the future as work continues on the border fence and related actions.

Members of Congress said that the input they were receiving from constituents showed that Americans were highly skeptical that the government would follow through on its promises about tough enforcement of security measures after the amnesty in 1986 (see entry for November 6, 1986) was supposed to be coupled with tighter restrictions on the hiring of illegal immigrants and the tighter restrictions were essentially never enforced at all.

President Bush said he understood such skepticism, and he offered to sign an agreement that the United States Treasury set aside $4.4 billion to pursue the border fence and workplace enforcement measures. The money would be repaid in the future from fines collected from illegal immigrants who go through the legalization process. An additional agreement that each side would offer only about 11 more amendments during the debate on the bill gave new hope that the Senate might actually vote on a bill by the end of June.

June 26, 2007 — The Senate passed a procedural vote to begin debate once again on an immigration bill. However, support for the bill seemed to be declining. Generally, some observers felt that within the country there was evidence that a line had been crossed where "immigration," an issue looked on generally in a favorable way, had finally been clearly separated in people's minds from "illegal immigration," an issue looked upon in a distinctly unfavorable way.

June 28, 2007 — The Senate refused to end debate on the Immigration Bill, a move that essentially doomed the bill for this session of Congress, and maybe more sessions to come. The highly praised strategy of the "Gang of 12" that had overseen the writing of the complicated legislation and nursed it through the Senate seemed in retrospect to be little more than an attempt to push it rapidly through the Senate before it could be defeated by the amendment writing process. It was a vote to end debate that ended in failure on June 7, 2007 (see entry), and it was the same kind of vote that killed it today. The bill never got to the point of having a simple "yea or nay" vote on its merits.

In hindsight observers said this seemed a strange strategy to try in the Senate which has a number of rules that permit even a single Senator to delay a piece of legislation. But the bill was so complex that its only chance may have seemed to go with all deliberate speed and hope grassroots support would bring pressure to pass it. But the main message from the grassroots was no more amnesty and a new (honest) effort to enforce the laws now on the books. The 1986 bill (see entry for November 6, 1896) was used as a comparison where the government had provided amnesty and promised new laws to stop illegal immigration in the future. However, the 1986 laws were not only inadequate, there was no honest attempt to enforce them. In fact, there were cynical modifications in favor of agricultural interests to be sure the new restrictive laws could not be readily enforced at work sites.

This time millions of American people stated clearly to their Congressional representatives that they did not want a repeat of 1986, but they did want active enforcement of the laws on the books. A sea change had occurred in favor to enforce law against illegal immigration, and perhaps it had been heightened by the tone of the debate in the Senate. People generally did not see any "grand bargain" in the exchange of tighter border security for what they saw as amnesty. They asked why not simply have better border security and its benefits without any further gifts for illegal aliens?

There was discussion about trying to pass parts of the immigration bill piecemeal, but the first consensus seemed to be that a simpler approach would be to actively enforce the laws on the books. It may well be that the most recent four months of 2007 will be the last time for several years that discussions of benefits for illegal immigrants are heard in Washington, D.C. Accordingly, the immigration law of 2000, passed seven years ago (see entry for 2000), could be the last to offer additional benefits for illegal immigrants in this decade or the next. The one thing proven by the long and tortuous process of the rise and fall of the proposed immigration bill of 2007 is that there is presently no consensus in favor of helping illegal immigrants in any way. The only real consensus is the one in favor of stopping illegal immigration into the United States for good, and deporting those caught in the process of trying illegally to work within the United States. As noted, June of 2007 marked the clear arrival of a great sea change against illegal immigration in the United States.

July 25, 2007— Demonstrating the great anger building in Congress over issues associated with illegal immigration, the house passed a bill trying to essentially free two Border Patrol agents imprisoned for shooting and wounding a fleeing drug smuggler in 2005. The former judge, Rep. Ted Poe, who sponsored an amendment denying the use of federal funds to keep the agents in prison, was especially outraged that the border agents were prosecuted rather than the illegal drug smugglers.

It is not clear how far the bill will progress with this amendment as many think it sets a bad precedent, and there were bipartisan calls for President Bush to commute the sentences of the agents to resolve the issue in a better way. But the action in the house was another indicator that any legislation seen in any way as being favorable to illegal immigrants was not likely to pass the present Congress.

July 26, 2007— United States District Judge James M. Munley struck down the Hazelton, Pennsylvania ordnance taking actions against illegal immigrants. The ordnance gained much attention in 2006 (see entry for August 22, 2006) as one of the first of its kind barring businesses from renting to or employing illegal immigrants. Many other communities across the United States followed with individual actions of their own against illegal immigrants.

Judge Manley based his decision on the usual basis that only the federal government can take actions to regulate immigration, but he added the additional stipulation that even people who enter the country illegally are protected by the "due process of law" section of the 14th Amendment of the Constitution. Opponents to the Hazelton ordnance hailed the decision, and said it would end such actions everywhere in the United States. Supporters of the issue said they would appeal to the Supreme Court, who they felt would reverse Judge Manley's decision.

The issue seems likely to continue in the courts as the National Conference of State Legislatures said in the first four months of 2007 alone, 1,169 bills and resolutions concerning immigration were introduced in state legislatures, compared with 570 bills introduced in 2006. Local communities already passing or discussing ordnances similar to that of Hazelton are estimated to number 1,200 according to the Federation for American Immigration Reform (FAIR). One critic said that country was burning with immigration issues while Congress did its usual partisan fiddling.

July 27, 2007— The Senate and the House put the finishing touches on a bill concerning the new budget for the Department of Homeland Security (DHS). Among many other things, the bill included an extra three billion dollars for more fencing along the border with Mexico, more border agents, and other enforcement measures to gain "operational control" over the southern border of the United States within two years. In essence, the presence in the United States of a large number of illegal immigrants near border areas is an indication that many people are crossing the border with no screening of any type, which means they can bring anything — and anybody — they wish into the country. Increased border control is meant to prevent this.

The border security issues were basically lifted from the proposed immigration bill that failed in the Senate on June 28, 2007 (see entry). President Bush has threatened to veto any bills that exceed his budget plan, as this one does, but the bill has overwhelming support and the President was seen as unlikely to use a veto that could be overridden on a bill containing the key security issues this one does.

This bill represents the first incremental piece of the failed "comprehensive" immigration legislation of last month. Not surprisingly, this particular incremental piece addressed the issue of border security. Congress learned last month that border security was one of the few popular parts of the comprehensive bill. As manufacturers realize that security, including ways of determining the legal status of workers, is actually going to be tightened, the feeling was that various industries may press for improved temporary worker programs to provide needed workers. Such a request could lead to another incremental piece of immigration legislation, but only if the suggestion of any sort of amnesty is absolutely avoided.

If the border security bill is strictly enforced, including the deportation of workers found to be in the United States illegally, observers commented that the large increase in illegal immigration of the past two decades could be halted, and their numbers may actually begin a slow decline. At any rate, this bill, assuming it passes, will represent the first time that a bill specifically targeting the issue of ending illegal immigration, has had broad popular support.

August 2, 2007 — A group of Republican Senators, led by John Kyl of Arizona, introduced a bill to tighten enforcement of immigration laws throughout the country. Kyl was a key member of the group that tried but failed to pass a comprehensive immigration bill in June (see entry for June 28, 2007), and as predicted then, his new bill picked up on the security issues of the failed bill and added some other issues in an attempt to pass them piecemeal.

The new bill would make it easier for border agents to seize smuggler's cars at the border, mandate jail time for people who overstay their visas (a category estimated to account for 40 percent of all illegal immigrants), and use closed military bases as detention centers. The bill does not classify illegal immigrants as felons as did the tough House bill of December 2005 (see entry for December 16, 2005), but the new bill would make fraudulent use of a Social Security number a felony. Because many illegal immigrants have done exactly that, they would be barred from any new legalization programs that may develop in the future.

The bill was co-sponsored by Kyl, Lindsay Graham of South Carolina, John McCain of Arizona, and Jeff Sessions of Alabama. This is an influential group of Senators and makes it likely the bill will see additional action. Kyl stated he didn't expect the bill to pass in its present form, but he did expect it to be used as a model for future bills. It was another step in the growing sentiment in Congress towards stricter enforcement of laws targeting illegal immigrants.

August 3, 2007 — Reports were circulating through Washington, D.C., that the Department of Homeland Security (DHS) was about to issue a notice outlining what steps employers must take when they receive a letter pointing out that there are discrepancies between the files of Social Security and what their employee reports under the Social Security number the employee claims to have obtained.

This is not a new issue (such letters have been sent since 1979), but what is new is that the employer must now take some action rather than ignoring the letter. As in almost everything involved with illegal immigration, employers mostly have been ignoring their obligations for the two decades since amnesty was granted for illegal immigrants in 1986 (see entry for November 6, 1986) and Congress said (with fingers crossed behind their backs) that future illegal immigrants would be deterred by laws forbidding the hiring of illegal immigrants. Such laws were never fully enforced, producing more than four times as many illegal immigrants today than were granted amnesty under the terms of the 1986 law. This blatant duplicity was also a prime cause of the failure of the new immigration reforms in June of this year when many citizens told their representatives in Congress frankly that they simply didn't believe the government would do what they claimed they were going to do relative to the enforcement of the new immigration law.

Now that era of honest enforcement of immigration laws has suddenly arrived, employers and other illegal immigration advocates have suddenly panicked at the thought they will now have to do what they should have been doing during the last two decades. The fact that employers have been blithely ignoring the law for so long with no consequences is indicative of the way the government basically conspired with employers to ignore the laws of 1986 and went on doing it for two decades.

The outcries from groups representing industries such as farming, restaurants, construction, janitorial, and landscaping services regarding impending doom in their areas of business are simply admissions that they have been illegally hiring illegal immigrants for decades, and that they know it very well in spite of the game they have been playing by saying they have not been "knowingly" hiring illegal immigrants. This was their way of avoiding penalties. Obviously they know which employees are illegal immigrants if they plead they will lose many employees if laws against hiring them are enforced.

In 2005, 8.1 million letters were sent to employees asking them to resolve discrepancies, and 1.5 million were directed to employers where no employee addresses were available. Another kind of letter was sent to 138,000 employers who had 10 or more employees with discrepancies. As noted, the issue is not new. What is new is that employers must fire such workers whose discrepancies are not resolved within 90 days. As noted, the outcry from employers that this would devastate their work forces easily identifies those who have, quite knowingly, hired illegal immigrants during more than the last 20 years. Some observers have noted that finally making up for decades of ignoring the law is inevitably bound to cause pain and disruptions for many people in many industries. The era of honest enforcement of the immigration laws has begun, and much of the fallout will be unpleasant at the beginning of the process.

August 10, 2007— The head of the Department of Homeland Security (DHS), Michael Chertoff, along with the Secretary of Commerce, Carlos M. Gutierrez, took the lead in announcing the actions being taken by the Bush administration to enforce the immigration laws. The primary new information had to do with enforcement in the workplace and the identification of illegal immigrants using fraudulent Social Security numbers and those employers who illegally hired them, but there were also discussions about border security and improved guest worker programs.

Representative Brian P. Bilbray of California commented that such steps were exactly what the American people had been waiting for. If they could see that the federal government was finally going to keep its word about enforcing the immigration laws, then maybe some other parts of the failed immigration bill of June 7, 2007 (see entry) could also be enacted. Other pro-immigrant officials said that it was estimated that half of the nation's 2.5 million agricultural workers were illegal immigrants (some estimate up to 70 percent) and thus the crackdown could be devastating to the supply of agricultural products.

Chertoff stated he had little sympathy for employers of any kind who hire illegally, and both he and Gutierrez commented that they hoped the enforcement actions and resulting difficulties would stimulate Congress to take some additional immigration actions. Gutierrez said specifically that "we do not have the workers our economy needs to keep our economy growing each year," and he and other observers saw the need for improved guest worker programs.

Others have pointed out in the past that Congress has simply lacked the political will to increase the issuance of enough legal immigration visas to the level the nation actually needs, and the anticipated lack of workers if the illegal immigrant enforcement efforts succeed may finally trigger Congress to take some positive action that rises above partisan politics.

August 25, 2007 — Tamar Jacoby, a senior fellow at the Manhattan Institute, who often writes about immigration issues, mentioned in an article that a recent Rasmussen poll showed eight in 10 Americans (80 percent) were in favor on the present crackdown on employers who hire illegal immigrants and in favor of the present emphasis on enforcing the immigration laws. This represents a dramatic reversal of the often vague statements made by proponents of the failed "comprehensive" immigration reform bill that "over 50 percent" of Americans favored their bill.

Jacoby was concerned about the severe affects the enforcement effort, if successful, could have on the economy, especially in California, the prime supplier of fruits and vegetables to the nation. Jacoby stated that the upcoming economic disruption in many industries could have a "silver lining" if it goaded Congress into developing new laws that would permit the importation of many more foreign workers in legal ways that has been the case in the past, a position Jacoby has long espoused, but she wasn't optimistic that Congress (and the American public) would find the political will to finally do the right thing.

September 17, 2007 — Reports circulated throughout Washington, D.C., that some members of Congress were going to try to pass some immigration bills piecemeal as a way to get their favorite immigration legislation enacted. This was in spite of the fact that there was no hope of reviving the comprehensive immigration act that was so soundly defeated in June (see entry for June 28, 2007).

One example was the "Dream Act" championed by Democratic Senator Richard J. Durbin of Illinois. This bill would grant conditional legal status to children of illegal immigrants who were brought to the United States at a young age, and who could become legal permanent residents if they met certain conditions over time. The bill was claimed to have broad support, but not so broad that Durbin would try to get it passed on its own. He hoped to attach it as an amendment to a defense funding measure scheduled to come before the Senate this week.

Similarly, Senator Dianne Feinstein of California planned to pursue a bill for a "blue visa" that she presented in January of this year (see entry for January 10, 2007) that would permit immigrants to come to the United States to perform agricultural work and eventually seek legalization under certain conditions. The bill is called an AgJobs program because it aimed at providing workers for agricultural interests. Again, even though it has other supporters, Feinstein planned to try to attach it as an amendment to the farm bill due for debate later in the fall.

Both bills have opponents lining up to oppose them. It has been pointed out that the bills, if passed as they stand, would essentially grant what is considered amnesty to four million illegal immigrants. That is about a third of the total the failed immigration bill tried to grant amnesty to back in June.

Senator Mel Martinez of Florida, who was part of the group supporting the comprehensive bill in June, and who is the only Senator to have been an immigrant himself, is opposed to the piecemeal approach. He stated that doing "the easy things" reduces the pressure on Congress to attack the "hard things" in immigration.

Observers noted that there is certainly a need to try to increase the number of temporary workers admitted under any immigration plan, but the attitude of enforcement over any sort of amnesty still appears to define the mood in Congress. The bills offering some sort of amnesty are forecasted to have tough sledding ahead, no matter how deeply they are buried in other bills.

Appendix 1:
Immigration by Decade

Figure 1.1 shows total immigration into the United States by decade from 1820, the first year official records of immigration were kept, to 2006, the last year for which data is available. An estimate is also made for the years from 2007 through 2009 based on results so far in the first years of the 21st century. The totals in Figure 1.1 may differ slightly from those of other sources because many sources chose to define the decade of the 1920s, for example, as 1921 through 1930, while Figure 1.1 shows the decade of the 1920s as a more logical 1920–1929. In this case the decade of the 1920s includes all 10 years numbered as 192x, with 1930 moved to the decade of the 1930s.

A total of 71.9 million legal immigrants were admitted to the United States in the 187 years from 1820 through 2006. The seven years from 2000 through 2006 have averaged just over one million legal immigrants per year, making it probable that the ten years from 2000 through 2009 will total 10 million legal immigrants, the highest decade total in the history of the United States. This record is even more significant considering that the second highest decade total is 9.8 million for the 1990s, and the decade of the 1990s, using the bookkeeping protocols of the then Immigration and Naturalization Service (INS), includes most of the about 2.7 million illegal immigrants that were granted amnesty by the 1986 Immigration Reforms.

Thus, the highest level of legal immigration into the United States

Appendix 1

Figure 1.1 — Immigration to the United States by Decade

Decade	Millions	Decade	Millions	
1820–29	0.1	1920–29	4.3	
1830–39	0.6	1930–39	0.7	
1840–49	1.4	1940–49	0.9	
1850–59	2.8	1950–59	2.5	
1860–69	2.1	1960–69	3.2	
1870–79	2.7	1970–79	4.2	
1880–89	5.2	1980–89	6.2	
1890–99	3.7	1990–99	9.8	
1900–09	8.2	2000–09	10.0	estimated
1910–19	6.3	2000–06	7.0	actual to date

Total	1820–2006	71.9 million	
Total	1820–2009	74.9 million estimated	
Total	1820–2009	89 million estimated including illegal immigrants	

Source: Department of Homeland Security

is taking place in the first decade of the 21st century, not back in some dusty time in the early 1900s as is often thought to be the case. The level of illegal immigrants in the country today as of roughly 2008 is generally thought to be about 12 million. If that value is added to the total of legal immigrants shown, total overall immigration into the United States as of today is about 84 million since 1820. Total immigration including legal and illegal immigrants will probably be about 87 million by 2009. A "typical" increase in the number of illegal immigrants between 2007 and 2009 would push the total immigrant flow since 1820 to about an astounding 89 million. And over 30 million of that number will have arrived in the last two decades.

The relatively "huge" surge of 8.2 million immigrants that took place in 1900–1909, and the over 17 million immigrants arriving in 1900–1924 triggered a series of restrictive immigration laws starting in 1917. They reached their most restrictive level with the 1924 Act that some historians saw as the "end of immigration." The restrictions were actually based on the new sources of immigrants after 1899 as much or more than the higher numbers (see Appendix 2). As the 1924 Act phased in, immigration fell sharply in the 1930s and 1940s. Of course the Great Depression of the 1930s and World War II in the 1940s also contributed to that decline.

Immigration totals began to rise again in the 1950s and 1960s as terms like War Brides, Displaced Persons, Refugees, and Asylum Seekers became common and the advent of the United Nations brought a new emphasis on the latter terms. But the single biggest influence on growing immigration totals after 1970 was the Immigration Act of 1965 that brought a civil rights perspective to immigration, and changed both the number and, most dramatically, the sources of immigration into the United States.

Steady liberalization of immigration laws produced steady growth of immigrants after the 1970s, and 1986 saw the granting of amnesty to about 2.7 million illegal immigrants. This act not only created 2.7 "new" legal immigrants, it led to an influx of new illegal immigrants that continues to this day. Each of the 2.7 million illegal immigrants granted amnesty under the terms of the 1986 law is estimated to have been replaced by four new illegal immigrants as of today. The 1986 amnesty was accompanied by a new law making it officially unlawful for employers to hire illegal immigrants, but the law was so blatantly ignored and ineffective, both in its creation and its implementation, that it actually attracted new illegal immigrants rather than preventing them. The illegal immigrants saw that no matter what the law said, they were welcome with open arms to continue working in the United States, and their best strategy was to continue pouring into the United States and await the next amnesty.

The 1986 amnesty and continued liberalization of the immigration laws through the 1990s and into 2000 produced the then record high of 9.8 million legal immigrants in the decade of the 1990s. However, the terrorist attacks of 2001 caused immigration to be looked at in a new light, that of a security issue. The highly liberalized immigration laws as of 2000 meant that yearly legal immigration totals continued to grow in the first decade of the 21st century (reaching, as noted, an average of over one million immigrants a year for the first seven years from 2000 through 2006), but a strong anti-illegal immigrant attitude developed in spite of, or maybe partly because of, an aggressive campaign by immigration advocates and immigrants themselves for the "right" of illegal immigrants to enter the United States as they wish.

This conflict came to a head in June of 2007, when the new Democratic Senate tried to pass a bill giving illegal immigrants the new amnesty

Appendix 1

they (and many others) expected was coming. There was basically a revolt in parts of the country against a new amnesty, and the duplicity the government had practiced for at least the last two decades in pretending to enforce the laws associated with the 1986 amnesty finally came home to roost. Many Americans said they simply didn't trust the government to carry out the new security inducements offered to get the amnesty part of the bill passed, and further they were outraged that some sort of special trade-offs were needed to enforce the security laws already on the books.

The Senate bill went down to a crushing defeat, and the attitude in Washington, D.C., changed to one of enforcement of immigration laws. Bills were enacted separately to give the Department of Homeland Security (DHS) extra money to fund essentially the same security issues contained in the defeated Senate bill, and the DHS showed a new aggressiveness in enforcing actions against employers who were breaking the law by hiring illegal immigrants. The era of enforcement seemed to have suddenly arrived.

Legal immigration is expected to continue growing in accordance with existing laws, and there may even be extra growth as new laws are developed to make up for the anticipated loss of illegal immigrants from the workforce. All of these items are discussed in the chronology, but the immigration data shown in Figure 1.1 is unable to show the effect of anti-illegal immigration laws on total immigration because no official record of illegal immigration exists. It is now clear that the focus of immigration today will be on dealing with illegal immigration. There will certainly be some adjustments needed on both sides to do this well. Even the illegal immigrants can claim a sense of "deception" in that after over 20 years of almost grateful acceptance in our economy, they are being told that not only are they not wanted, they will be prosecuted for what they have been doing for years. Enforcement of the law is certainly the correct thing to, but much of the pain could have been avoided if it had been enforced from day one.

Appendix 2: Immigration by Period and Source

Figure 2.1 shows immigration to the United States by the time period in which the immigrants came and the primary sources from which they came in each period. The total number of legal immigrants who arrived in each period is also shown.

The periods are defined as 1820–1849, when immigration to the United States was just beginning; 1850–1899 when the first big wave of immigrants arrived; 1900–1939, when immigration became so large (and from less desirable sources) that the infamous restrictive acts of the early 1920s were enacted to discourage immigration; 1940–1969 when immigration largely consisted of the fallout from World War II; and 1970–1999 when the famous immigration reforms of 1965 finally took effect and ultimately increased immigration to new highs and created completely new primary sources.

In the period of 1820–1849, immigration totaled only 2.1 million, with most of that coming in the 1840s when the potato blight caused famine in overcrowded Ireland and produced the beginning of an exodus that totaled about half the population of the island by the end of the century. Immigrants from Germany had already been coming to what became the United States in significant numbers since revolutionary times, and thus the Irish contributed 42 percent of the immigrants in 1820–1849, with the Germans making up 22 percent. The region of Europe thus sent 89 percent of all immigrants in 1820–1849, while the "Americas" (essentially all of the Western Hemisphere except the United States) sent 4 percent.

Appendix 2

Figure 2.1 — Immigration by Period and Region or Country of Origin

Period	1820–49	1850–99	1900–39	1940–69	1970–99
Years	30	50	40	30	30
Total in Period (Millions)	2.1	16.5	19.5	6.6	20.2
By Region					
Europe	89%	91%	79%	45%	14%
Americas	4%	7%	17%	45%	49%
Asia	—	2%	4%	9%	35%
By Country					
Ireland	42%	17%			
Germany	22%	26%		13%	
Italy			19%		
Russia			14%		
Canada				14%	
Mexico				12%	22%

In the 1850–1899 period, immigration boomed to 16.5 million as the era of the Industrial Revolution in the United States (featuring the railroads) created a great need for labor to build the expanding economy and to feed all its participants. The Germans made up 26 percent of the massive immigration, while the Irish added 17 percent. Europe provided 91 percent, the Americas seven percent, and Asia two percent in spite of intense discrimination against Asians.

In the 1900–1939 period, immigration soared to 19.5 million in ten fewer years than 1850–1899, with most of the new record total coming between 1900 and 1925. This huge crush of immigrants, and the fact that they came primarily from central and southern Europe rather than northern and western Europe as it had before, triggered the restrictive acts of 1924 and the years just before. Immigration in the 1930s fell back to the levels of the 1830s, due to the combination of the implementation of the new restrictive laws of the 1920s and the arrival of the Great Depression.

In the 1900–1939 period, Italians, who began immigrating in substantial numbers just before 1900, made up 19 percent of all immigrants. Part of this was due to intense promotion from the United States and the availability of much more rapid and comfortable steamship service across the Atlantic. Similar incentives applied to the Russians, largely eastern

European Jews, who provided the next highest number of immigrants at 14 percent.

As a region, Europe still supplied the highest number of immigrants at 79 percent, even if the core of their immigrants were from different parts of Europe than before. The Americas increased to 17 percent (the majority from Canada and Mexico), and Asia crept up to 4 percent (primarily from Japan and Turkey).

Immigration continued at very low levels in the 1940–1969 period. It wasn't until 1965 that the restrictive Act of 1924 was fully reversed, and the new 1965 reforms were not fully implemented until 1968. The effects of World War II and the urging by the new United Nations to honestly implement agreements having to do with Displaced Persons, Refugees, and seekers of Asylum made up much of the immigration activity. This led to Europe and the Americas each providing 45 percent of the immigrants to the United States in the period, with Asia now climbing to 9 percent. By country, Canada, Germany, and Mexico led a nearly three-way tie in what was basically a low period of immigration.

The 1970–1999 period marked the true flowering of immigration into the United States. The Civil Rights flavor of the 1965 law brought immigrants literally from all over the world. As explained in Appendix 4, certain aspects of the 1965 law also led to a large increase in illegal immigration, and that large increase became a flood after the defects of the 1986 law granting amnesty to existing illegal immigrants were fully exploited. Thus, the 1970–1999 period saw historical highs not only in legal immigration, but also in the uncounted number of illegal immigrants.

Legal immigration in the 1970–1999 period totaled a record high of 20.2 million, including the highest single year ever of 1.83 million in 1991 (when many of the 2.7 million illegal immigrants grated amnesty were officially counted). This made the 1990s the highest decade ever at 9.8 million (but the decade of 2000–2009 will likely surpass that total even without the aid of illegal immigrants becoming legal immigrants on the books as is shown in Appendix 1).

The amnesty of 1986 gave Mexico (Mexicans made up 70 percent of all amnesty applicants) a commanding lead as the top country providing the most immigrants in the 1970–1999 period with 22 percent of the legal immigration total (in 1991 Mexico provided an astronomical 52 percent of the total). But even in years without the benefit of amnesty bookkeeping, Mexico has typically provided a leading percentage in the high teens, with various Asian countries coming in second at percentages of 6 percent or below. Many, many other countries fill out the list with much lower percentages. This has been true for most of the 1970–1999 period, and is continuing into the new century.

For example, from 2000 through 2006, Mexico led as a source of immigrants at 17 percent, while India showed just over 6 percent and the Philippines and China showed a little under 6 percent each. And it must be remembered that all of this data refers to legal immigration. Mexico has been considered mostly as a source of illegal immigration recently, but for more than the past three decades, it has been far and away the leading source of legal immigration as well.

Because of Mexico's leading contribution, the Americas were the leading region as a source of legal immigrants with 49 percent for the 1970–1999 period. Asia, with all legal restrictions removed by the 1965 reforms, accounted for 35 percent of all immigrants in the 1970–1999 period. Europe, the leading source of immigrants from 1820 through 1969, provided only 14 percent in 1970–1999. This reversal of immigrant sources will probably continue into the foreseeable future assuming the present immigration laws remain essentially unchanged.

One other note should be made about Mexico's leading role in providing both legal and illegal immigrants to the United States in recent decades. Mexico has now passed Germany, Italy, Ireland, and Great Britain as a leading source of legal immigrants to the United States in the history of immigration. If, in fact, there are 12 million illegal immigrants now in the United States, and they are in the same proportion as the applicants for amnesty in 1986, then about 15 million Mexicans have immigrated to the United States in recent decades, and almost half of them are legal immigrants. If by some miracle the 12 million illegal immigrants now thought to be living in the United States are removed or leave by the end of the decade, Mexico will still be the leading country identified as their birthplace by the nation's foreign-born, and Mexico will still add to its lead as the country supplying the most legal immigrants yearly to the United States (by a factor of three).

Immigration by Period and Source

Regardless of how the struggle over illegal immigration is finally resolved, the contribution of people and their culture by Mexico to the United States will go on as it has for more than three decades, and the difference between legal and illegal immigrant will hopefully become primarily a thing of the past.

Appendix 3: Key Legislation Affecting Immigration

This appendix lists key legislation that had a significant effect on immigration in the United States. It is not intended to list all immigration laws, but only legislation that proved to shape immigration in an important and lasting way.

1849— The United States Supreme Court ruled in the so-called "Passenger Cases" that only the federal government can regulate immigration under the commerce clause of the Constitution. The case grew out of attempts by cities such as New York and Boston to charge fees on immigrants to help defray the costs of processing them. In a manner much different than today, the federal government did finally pick up the ball handed to them by the Supreme Court in 1849, establishing its own fees to cover costs and eventually building Ellis Island.

But this rather obscure case is the basis for today's heated arguments over the perceived failure of the federal government to stop illegal immigration, while courts block any individual, community, or state efforts to do so. The position of the courts is that, based on this 1849 ruling, only the federal government can act in this area, whether or not it has the political will to do so.

1868— The Secretary of State declared that the 14th Amendment, written in 1866, had been ratified by the proper number of states and was now part of the Constitution. The 14th Amendment was intended to protect the newly freed slaves in the south from any sort of discrimination by the governments of any of the states. For many decades Southern states managed by various means to get around this amendment and install a fully segregated society. However, the "Brown" school decision of 1954 essentially ended that process, and the "equal protection under the law" part of the 14th Amendment became a bulwark of civil rights, becoming more liberally interpreted and applied to many more situations then ever before.

One of those situations was the rights of illegal immigrants in the United States. Basically the courts have consistently ruled that the act of illegally entering the country does not strip illegal immigrants of their right to receive the protections of the 14th Amendment. This has led to requirements that states must provide illegal immigrants with a free public education, appropriate free medical care, and other non-discriminatory services. Famous examples include the 1982 Texas school case and California's Proposition 187 in 1994 as listed below.

But critics have pointed out that the Passenger Case of 1849, combined with the present interpretations of the 14th Amendment, have left Americans in a kind of "catch 22." If one sees illegal immigrants coming across the border, the Passenger Case forbids taking any non-federal action to prevent it. When the illegal immigrants arrive in town, the 14th Amendment requires providing them with a free education, appropriate free medical care, and being sure not to take any actions that could be considered discriminatory in terms of how regular citizens are treated. There is little wonder, critics further note, that as the number of illegal immigrants has grown to large numbers, the frustrations their presence engenders have grown as well. This explains in part the "revolt" that killed the immigration reform bill proposed in the Senate in 2007.

1924 — Long before the issue of illegal immigration became the prime focus of immigration laws, the 1924 Immigration Act, also known as the Johnson-Reed Act, installed quotas into the immigration law. The intention of the quotas was not only to reduce total immigration, but to reduce immigration from what was considered the undesirable ethnic areas of central, eastern, and southern Europe. The quotas favored those coming from northern and Western Europe (Asians were almost totally barred). The law was so harsh that it was called the "end of immigration" by future historian and author Oscar Handlin, who bemoaned as late as the end of the 1950s the failure to modify the 1924 act in what he considered any significant way, brushing aside the changes made to facilitate refugees from World War II as "temporary."

The 1924 act has stood as a symbol of everything future writers of immigration law wanted to avoid, and also a symbol of the United States in its most isolationist mood. The next substantial reform in 1965, just a few years after Handlin's litany, changed literally everything.

1965— The Immigration Act of 1965, passed in a time of a great focus on civil rights, brought a civil rights flavor to immigration as well. The 1965 act abolished the quota/national origins established by the 1924 act and subsequent modifications; established a yearly limit up to 170,000 immigrants from outside the Western Hemisphere (with a limit of 20,000 per country); admitted immigrants on a first come, first qualified basis; established preferences for relatives of citizens, refugees, and those with special skills; and placed a limit of 120,000 immigrants yearly from the Western Hemisphere (which was less than from outside the Western Hemisphere) to make up for past discrimination.

The limits and preferences were rapidly changed in subsequent years, but they were always liberalized compared to prior years. As noted in Appendix 4 the 1965 changes had some unintended negative consequences which promoted the increase of illegal immigration from Mexico, but the 1965 act became the basis for a model comprehensive immigration act that was constantly liberalized during the rest of the 20th century.

1982— The Supreme Court of the United States issued a decision that brought the 14th Amendment to center stage in the growing debate over illegal immigration and ratcheted up the frustration many Americans were beginning to feel about the issue. In a case concerning the efforts of the state of Texas to withhold state funds from the education of illegal aliens, the Court ruled that the illegal immigrants, although admittedly not citizens, were certainly "people," and thus are afforded 14th Amendment protections.

This ruling was repeated in many situations dealing with illegal immigrants in the future, and was tested in California's proposition 187 in 1994, and most recently in 2007 in the ruling of the case of the city of Hazelton, Pennsylvania, trying to take action against a local influx of illegal immigrants. In 2007 the presiding judge felt required to remind everyone that the act of entering the country illegally does not strip an illegal immigrant of 14th Amendment protections. Advocates of the Hazelton action feel that with many other similar cases pending, at least one, if not necessarily theirs, seems certain to reach the Supreme Court on the basis that a review is needed of the concept that illegally entering the country carries no legal cost to the persons doing so.

1986— The now somewhat infamous Immigration Reform and Control Act of 1986 was passed by Congress. Described later as an "inside job" by some critics, the act granted amnesty to what eventually totaled 2.7 million illegal immigrants, who had to do essentially nothing more than fill out some forms to change from illegal immigrants to legal immigrants while continuing to do the same things they had been doing for years within the United States.

What some described as a "fig leaf" to make the action more palatable was an accompanying ruling that prohibited employers from "knowingly" hiring illegal immigrants. Members of Congress claimed this ruling would prevent illegal immigration in the future. As is known now, the ruling was a sham. The word "knowingly" was deliberately inserted to give employers a way out of any penalties under the law by claiming no knowledge of the fact the persons they hired were illegal immigrants, and stipulations were added to the law essentially forbidding immigration agents from questioning the legal status of agricultural workers.

The 1986 act was basically negotiated between Congress and large employers of illegal immigrants (hence the term "inside job" by some critics), and with little input from the public. In 2007, the duplicity inherent in the act was a substantial cause of the revolt that killed the proposed "comprehensive" immigration reform bill in the Senate. People stated frankly that based on the results of the 1986 bill, they now believed the federal government had no credibility relative to enforcement of immigration law. People simply did not believe the government would take the enforcement actions promised in exchange for a new round of amnesty.

Further, illegal immigrants soon realized in 1986 that their labor would be as welcome as ever in the United States, and their best strategy would be to pour into the United States and take their usual round of jobs until the inevitable next amnesty. For each illegal immigrant granted amnesty in 1986, four new illegal immigrants had taken their place by 2007. And their expectation of a new round of amnesty nearly came true.

1994— The frustrations caused by the influx of a growing number of illegal immigrants resulted in 57 percent of the California electorate passing Proposition 187, a measure intended to reduce the costs of trying to absorb illegal immigrants and their children. The proposition was declared unconstitutional after it passed, the courts using as a basis the usual combination of the 1849 and 1868 actions described at the beginning of this Appendix. The proposition was generally roundly disparaged outside California, but by 2006 and 2007 many other government entities had passed similar laws of their own as illegal immigration climbed to new heights.

2005— In December of 2005, the House of Representatives passed a bill that made the act of entering the United States illegally a felony, and criminalized those assisting illegal immigrants. There were many similar clauses, and building a fence at the Mexican border and greatly increasing the border patrol was made a priority. The Senate dismissed the House bill in the spring of 2006 as much too harsh, and proposed one of their own which the House dismissed as much too liberal. The two sides "compromised" on a bill addressing the need for a fence as the 2006 elections approached. The Democrats hoped to sweep the elections (which they did) and propose a new amnesty bill in 2007.

2007— The Democrats began considering their "comprehensive" immigration reform, but they sensed, as did others that the American people, although still favoring legal immigration, had turned against the flouting of the law (and potentially the security) of the country that was illegal immigration. Some Senators (and administration officials) went behind closed doors in a novel attempt to craft a bill that would meet the competing desires of more security and amnesty. But by June the once promising attempts to pass the bill had failed, and it soon appeared that immigration had entered a new phase of "Enforcement of the Law."

Appendix 4:
The *Bracero* Program

The *bracero* (a Mexican word used to describe contract laborers) program was started in 1942 when the United States and the Mexican governments agreed to bring Mexican laborers into the United States temporarily to work as railroad gangs and agricultural field hands. This would replace American workers leaving for service in World War II. The initial program lasted only until 1947, but there were various extensions until 1951, and then the Korean War brought more extensions and even expansions. The bracero program finally expired in 1964. But it turned out to have a significant long-term effect on illegal immigration, and thus it is discussed in detail in this appendix.

The beginning of World War II had a domino effect on Mexican laborers in the United States. In spite of the preceding depression, there were still many legal and illegal immigrants in the United States when the war broke out. However, these immigrants, typically working in rural areas, followed the money, so to speak, and moved to higher paying jobs in urban areas in airplane factories, shipyards, and other defense industries. These industries were desperate for labor as Americans joined the military. This in turn made agricultural centers in the rural areas desperate for labor. This condition triggered the bracero program in 1942.

More than 220,000 workers joined the program, with the Agriculture Department administering it and guaranteeing a minimum number of hours of work and suitable wages and living conditions. Over 21 states took part, although half of the braceros went to California (but none to Texas because the Mexican government felt Texas had demonstrated great discrimination towards Mexicans in the past).

The original program ended in 1947 as noted, but although there were the usual abuses in such a program, braceros were anxious to continue what for them were good wages, and southwestern growers were more than anxious to use the labor of the braceros. Program extensions were made, and even Texas was permitted to join. The program peaked in the late 1950s with over 400,000 workers taking part yearly.

Ironically, the bitter protests of Mexican-American workers who had already been in the United States prior to the bracero program helped to end it. The existing workers felt they were not being treated as well as the braceros, and with an election win by the Democrats in 1960, and help from organized labor which normally supported Democrats, the existing workers won their case and the bracero program was ended by 1964. In 1965, the great immigration reform bill with a focus on civil rights was passed and efforts like the bracero program were forgotten.

However, almost five million braceros had entered the United States during the bracero program from 1942 through 1964, and southwestern growers had begun to depend on their labor. Many illegal immigrants from Mexico were also hired, and although a crackdown on illegal immigrants resulted in the deportation of about four million of them between 1947 and 1954, the relationship was well established between the southwestern growers and illegal immigrants. The use of illegal immigrants expanded and became the biggest source of labor in the southwestern United States economy.

In the meantime, Mexico was becoming the largest source of legal immigration into the United States (see Appendix 2), and a culture was established in the southwestern United States in which Mexican immigrants could feel at home even in the face of blatant discrimination. The amnesty of 1986 brought 2.7 million more legal Mexican immigrants to the United States by the simple process of labeling them "legal" rather than "illegal" as they stayed in place and kept doing what they had been doing for years.

When the illegal immigrants learned that the new law accompanying the 1986 amnesty to the effect that it was now illegal in the United

States to "knowingly" hire an illegal immigrant was a sham, illegal immigrants poured into the United States from both Mexico and countries to the south. About 30 percent of the illegal immigrants receiving amnesty per the 1986 law were from countries other than Mexico, and they, like the Mexicans, realized the best strategy was to get into the United States by any means and wait for the next amnesty. By 2007, an estimated 12 million illegal immigrants were awaiting the next amnesty.

It must be noted that the illegal immigrants in the United States may well feel they were misled. After over twenty years of being welcomed with open arms by employers in the United States, and after having only to avoid some border tightening that essentially made them try several times rather than just once to enter the United States, they find that suddenly the United States is preparing to enforce its long existing laws against illegal immigration. And although this may result in some modifications of existing immigration laws to permit the legal hiring of many temporary workers to replace illegal immigrant workers who are deported, it won't help the illegal immigrants who accepted what they thought was an invitation to find work and are now forever branded with the mark of "illegal immigrant." But it was a risk they decided to take, and it appears to be a strategy that failed.

Appendix 5:
Immigration and Population

Some individuals and groups are opposed to both legal and illegal immigration because of its impact on the environment. These persons believe that the population of the United States is growing much too rapidly, putting great pressure on the natural environment and on the overall resources of the country. They see the present rate of population growth being driven too high by both legal and illegal immigrants, and they wish to greatly decrease immigration of all types. this appendix addresses this issue and presents the relative facts and data.

The first problem those urging limits on population growth see is not just immigration to the United States per se, but total population growth in the world as a whole. However, that particular population issue has changed dramatically in recent years. In spite of various doomsday books projecting doublings of the earth's population far into the future with disastrous consequences, the rate of increase of the world's population began to diminish just as the most notorious of the doomsday books, *The Population Bomb*, was published in 1971. The most recent doubling of the earth's population took place between 1963 and 2006, when the momentum of prior population increases drove the population from about 3.25 billion in 1963 to 6.5 billion in 2007. Based on present estimates by the Department of the Census, the world's population should never double again from the 2006 baseline.

By 2050 the population of the world is estimated to reach 9.4 billion on the way to stabilizing somewhere short of 10 billion. Some experts think it may stabilize earlier when it stands below 9 billion. That's still a lot of people, but well below the almost frantic forecasts of only a few years ago. The most important fact is that the rate of increase has been declining on a regular basis since the 1990s and is forecasted to continue to do so indefinitely. Thus, any increase in the population of the United States will not be part of a runaway increase in the population of the world.

In fact, the present population problem in most developed countries of the world is not excessive population growth, but a forecasted population decline that is threatening to disrupt social payments (similar to our Social Security) from one generation to another. Previously rapidly growing countries like China and Brazil have taken actions to reduce their birthrates. China will actually lose population between 2025 and 2050, and Brazil will increase by less than 5 percent in that period. Between now and 2050, Japan and Russia will each lose over 20 percent of their populations, and most of Europe will see declines of 10 percent or more.

The United States is one of the few developed countries that will avoid a decline, and this is because of its present legal immigration rate of over one million per year. Analysts say it is not clear how high the population of such a highly developed, low density population country such as the United States can grow before seriously impacting the overall standard of living. The population of the United States grew by 86 percent in the fifty years between 1950 and 2000, and although many define the country as "too crowded," objectively the United States in 2000 was a better place to live than in 1950 in most ways by most measures. There is little reason to believe that an additional 40 percent increase in population between the 300 or so million of 2008 and about 420 million in 2050 will make the country "unlivable." But it will certainly be more crowded and will put further strains on the environment.

There is no doubt that the population increase between now and 2050 will be due to immigration. The book *Unguarded Gates* by Otis L. Graham shows that from a baseline of 203 million people in 1970, the United States would have peaked at about 255 million in 2020, and then have begun to decline to 236 million by 2050—if no immigration had taken place after 1970. But adding the immigrants since 1970 has produced a population of 300 million as of 2006 (an "extra" 50 million people), and will produce a population of 404 million by 2050 (an extra 168 million, and present projections increase the 404 million estimate in 2050 to 420 million). Advocates of limiting population find this very undesirable, but many developed nations around the world are presently trying to modify their immigration laws and giving bonuses to new mothers in an attempt to essentially emulate the "success" on the United States in avoiding population losses.

This is the crux of the debate over the impact of immigration on the population. Most developed countries find the resulting population increase desirable because it avoids an overall economic decline, and postpones the day of reckoning in the Social Security system where either benefits must be cut or taxes increased — or both. Either is a very unpalatable political decision. Immigration demographics are usually very favorable in that they add more working-age people than retirement-age people and thus further postpone unpleasant Social Security decisions. Thus, the impact of immigration on population is either favorable or unfavorable, depending on who you ask and what their priorities are. The most typical answer in the near future is likely to be that more immigration is better, as long as it is more immigration of the legal sort.

Appendix 6: Eugenics and the 1924 Immigration Act

This appendix discusses the effect of the then-popular pseudo-science of eugenics on the development of the very restrictive Immigration Act of 1924. It was an unfortunate combination of a movement that attempted to exclude certain racial and ethnic groups from immigrating to the United States by finding a so-called scientific validation for their otherwise clearly racist actions. Those who supported eugenics, including many prominent persons and institutions, were ultimately highly embarrassed by the extent of their actions.

Eugenics basically grew out of Charles Darwin's *The Origin of Species*, published amid great controversy in 1859. But once the concept of evolution took hold and was considered by many the modern, up-to-date way of looking at the world, it was not hard for many prominent and well-educated people to be led to believe that literally everything was an inherited trait, including culture, social patterns, and individual intelligence. Eugenics in many cases led in this direction, especially if used by certain people to create a "scientific" basis for their existing prejudices. In the worst case it led to the deadly practices of Adolph Hitler. On a less deadly but still despicable situation, eugenics helped support the writing of the basically racist Immigration Act of 1924.

The 1924 Immigration Act was the most restrictive immigration act ever written in the United States in terms of its overall effect on immigration. The Chinese Exclusion Act of 1882 was openly racist, and it totally barred Chinese immigrants from entering the United States. But it only affected relatively few immigrants in terms of the total entering the United States at the time. Other restrictive acts written near 1882 and after barred "prostitutes, convicts, lunatics, idiots, people likely to become a public charge, polygamists, anarchists, and other radicals," and so forth. But this long laundry list was not necessarily based on race or ethnicity, and it actually affected relatively few of the millions of immigrants pouring into the country at the time the laws were passed.

However, the 1924 Immigration Act affected millions of immigrants and potential immigrants at the time it was passed. The 1924 act stood as a symbol of isolation for almost three decades, and represented "the end of immigration" to some scholars. The degree to which the 1924 act was influenced by the pseudo-science of eugenics has been a matter of dispute since the act was developed and written, but most historians of eugenics have no doubt that the 1924 act was yet another victim of the nasty effects that resulted from the almost national craze that existed over eugenics, until eugenics was finally discredited when Hitler made it a centerpiece of his racist policies in the 1930s. The 1924 act did not so much try to reduce total immigration as it tried to reduce — or even eliminate — immigration from specific areas such as eastern and southern Europe and nearly all of Asia. Eugenics as practiced by many was the perfect partner for this task.

The so-called science of eugenics had a high level following in the United States from 1865 until the end of the 1920s. Eugenics is basically a social philosophy that advocates the selective breeding of human beings to improve certain traits and eliminate others. Such concepts go back to Plato, but the modern version was started in 1865 in England by Sir Francis Dalton, who was a cousin of Charles Darwin. Prominent people such as Alexander Graham Bell, George Bernard Shaw, Winston Churchill, and Theodore Roosevelt, among many others, became supporters of the idea.

In the United States, eugenics was a subject taught at many colleges and universities, and was underwritten by sources such as the Rockefeller Foundation, the Carnegie Institution of Washington, D.C., and the Harriman Family. Alexander Graham Bell, who originally studied deafness and hearing impairment (the invention of the telephone was an outgrowth of his experiments in improving hearing), concluded that deafness was a hereditary trait and proposed a ban on marriages involving deaf people, even though he had married a deaf student of his. Bell early on proposed banning deaf immigrants, and he suggested boarding schools for the deaf could be considered breeding places for a deaf human race.

There was basically no hard scientific evidence for such theories, but the prominence of people like Bell who proposed them gave them wide credence. Charles B. Davenport, a known American biologist, founded what was called the Station for Experimental Evolution in 1904 with funding from the Carnegie Institution. This was an example of how the eugenics movement tried to tie their work to the legitimate work of Darwin. This produced the Eugenics Record Office (ERO) in 1910, developed by Davenport and his colleague, Harry H. Laughlin. The ERO collected large amounts of data on family pedigrees, and concluded that most "unfit" people came from economically and socially poor backgrounds. The ERO pushed for immigration limits on such groups, while other eugenics followers wanted segregation, sterilization, or even extermination of "unfit" people.

Davenport wrote a book in 1911 titled *Heredity in Relation to Eugenics* which decried the great immigrant influx at the time from southern and eastern Europe as ultimately having a great negative effect of the "gene pool" and the future population of the United States. Davenport saw the "unnatural" extension of the life span by modern medicine of feeble minded and unfit people as a danger to society. His 1911 book became a college textbook for many years.

Harry H. Laughlin was characterized as an "expert" witness in 1920 by the Committee in the House of Representatives considering immigration bills, including those which resulted in the Immigration Act of 1924. Laughlin especially believed in compulsory sterilization of what he considered the unfit to keep them from infecting the future gene pool. Among other things, he testified before the House committee on the "excessive insanity" of immigrants from eastern and southern Europe, and produced, as usual, what he claimed to be appropriate statistical data from the ERO to support his claims.

Laughlin drafted a "model law" for compulsory sterilization for states to use so they could address constitutional and ethical issues in carrying out their sterilization programs. He published it in 1922 as part of his study of American sterilization policy. With Laughlin's help, more than

Appendix 6

60,000 Americans were sterilized under eugenic guidelines until the practice finally fell out of favor by the 1970s.

As noted earlier, a study made by some historians claimed that eugenics was not really the key to the 1924 act, and that Congress wished only to "maintain the country's cultural integrity against a heavy influx of foreigners." Considering that it was only the influx of certain races and ethnic groups that the 1924 act wished to exclude, and that inputs from such people as Harry Laughlin were considered "expert testimony," it is hard not to conclude, as most historians of eugenics have, that regardless of whatever code word were used, Congress fully intended to pass an immigration act in accordance with the tenets of eugenics, and that is just what it did.

Bibliography

This bibliography lists the key references consulted in completing this book. There are several excellent histories of immigration, but first it must be noted that with the substantial changes in immigration that have taken place in the United States in 2005 through 2007, especially with respect to illegal immigration, the conclusions of the books in the bibliography generally are unusually far off the mark. The biggest crisis in immigration in 2008 is certainly illegal immigration and how to deal with it, and most of these books refer to illegal immigration as simply "a vexing problem" or some similar phrase. At the time the books were written, the events of 2005 and after were not imagined.

When drawing a conclusion about the future of immigration to end their books, the authors of historical treatments tended to conclude that the future will be roughly "more of the same." That conclusion seemed justified by the relatively recent history of immigration. Even though books published not long ago noted what seem to them indicators of substantial change, these indicators were brushed off. But a substantial change in attitude towards illegal immigration has, in fact, taken place, and it is very unlikely it will ever return to what it was.

With this disclaimer, the two books by Roger Daniels, and the books by Maldyn Jones and Leonard Dinnerstein and David Reimers are especially good comprehensive histories of immigration up to the date they were written. There is little in the history of immigration that is not well documented in these books. One would hope that someone of the quality of these authors would take up the challenge to write about the dramatic changes in immigration that have taken place since 2001. Then they could try to determine how these changes will play out in the near future.

This situation underlines the need to depend on the Internet as a key reference source in completing any book. In the world of today, the Internet has to be used as a major source in any research activity, and much use was made of it in this book. As before, no attempt is made to note the many contributions the Internet has made because those contributions usually take the form of a compilation of facts drawn from multiple Internet entries and modified and updated for use in this book as appropriate.

Selected Bibliography

Barkan, Elliot Robert. *And Still They Come: Immigrants and the American Society.* The American History Series. Wheeling, IL: Harlan Davidson, Inc., 1996.

Bridgewater, William, and Seymour Kurtz, eds. *The Columbia Encyclopedia.* 3rd ed. New York: Columbia University Press, 1963.

Daniels, Roger. *Coming to America: A History of Immigration and Ethnicity in American Life.* 2nd ed. New York: HarperCollins, 2002.

_____. *Guarding the Golden Door: American Immigration Policy and Immigrants since 1882.* New York: Hill and Wang, 2004.

Dinnerstein, Leonard, and David M. Reimers. *Ethnic Americans: A History of Immigration.* 4th ed. New York: Columbia University Press, 1999.

Dublin, Thomas, ed. *Immigrant Voice: New Lives in America, 1773–1986.* Chicago: University of Illinois Press, 1993.

Foner, Nancy. *From Ellis Island to JFK: New York's Two Great Waves of Immigration.* New Haven, CT: Russell Sage Foundation, 2000.

Graham, Otis L., Jr. *Unguarded Gates: A History of America's Immigration Crisis.* Lanham, MD: Rowman & Littlefield Publishers, 2006.

Handlin, Oscar. *Immigration as a Factor in American History.* Englewood Cliffs, NJ: Prentice-Hall, 1959.

_____. *The Uprooted: The Epic Story of the Great Migrations That Made the American People.* New York: Grosset & Dunlap, 1951.

Jones, Maldwyn Allen. *American Immigration.* 2nd ed. Chicago: The University of Chicago Press, 1992.

Kashner, Zoe, editorial director. *The World Almanac and Book of Facts, 2007.* New York: World Almanac Education Group, 2007.

Laxton, Edward. *The Famine Ships: The Irish Exodus to America.* New York: Henry Holt and Company, LLC, 1998.

Ngai, Mae M. *Impossible Subjects: Illegal Aliens and the Making of Modern America.* Princeton, NJ: Princeton University Press, 2004.

Portes, Alejandro, and Ruben G. Rumbaut. *Immigrant America: A Portrait.* 3rd ed., revised. Berkeley: University of California Press, 2006.

Wright, Russell O. *Chronology of Education in the United States.* Jefferson, NC: McFarland, 2006.

_____. *Chronology of the Stock Market.* Jefferson, NC: McFarland, 2002.

Index

Index

Index

Index

Index

Index